HEATHERLEY

Flora Thompson

When the young Flora Thompson took up her duties at Grayshott post-office in 1898, she found to her amazement that her customers included Arthur Conan Doyle and George Bernard Shaw. The neighbouring settlement of Hindhead had attracted many eminent Victorians to take up residence, and the telegraph machine at Grayshott which Flora was employed to operate was their prime means of communication to the outside world.

In *Heatherley*, she tells us that as a result of meeting these famous authors she 'destroyed her own scraps of writing, saying to herself as they smouldered to tinder that that was the end of a foolish idea.'

Fortunately it did not stop her altogether, and from the perspective of some forty-five years after the events described, Flora Thompson remembers with her usual clarity back to a time when bicycles and Kodak cameras were just becoming popular, and she herself was guilty of crossing the strict conventions of propriety at the end of the nineteenth century.

Introduction by Anne Mallinson.
Illustrations by Hester Whittle.
Historical notes by John Owen Smith.

D1028299

Cover illustration:—

Sandy tracks through heather and birch on Weavers Down, near Liphook—this was Flora's 'Peverel Down,' and typical of the scenery in East Hampshire with which she fell in love.

Photograph by John Owen Smith

Grandma.

Christmas 1999

love
Auntie, Steve Hannah + Harriet

HEATHERLEY

Flora Thompson

Heatherley

First published 1979 by Oxford University Press as part of
A Country Calendar and other writings, selected and edited by
Margaret Lane

This edition published September 1998 using original material
supplied by The Harry Ransom Humanities Research Center, The
University of Texas at Austin, whose assistance is acknowledged.

Reprinted 1999

Typeset and published by John Owen Smith
19 Kay Crescent, Headley Down, Hampshire GU35 8AH
Tel/Fax: 01428 712892
E-mail: wordsmith@headley1.demon.co.uk

© The Estate of Flora Thompson

Introduction © Anne Mallinson
Illustrations © Hester Whittle
Notes © John Owen Smith

ISBN 1-873855-29-X

Cover printed by Pier House Ltd, Bourne Mill, Farnham, Surrey

Text printed and bound by Antony Rowe Ltd, Bumper's Farm,
Chippenham, Wiltshire

Publisher's Note

In producing this new edition of *Heatherley* to mark the centenary of Flora's arrival in Hampshire, we have reviewed her original typescript alongside the version edited by Margaret Lane and previously published by Oxford University Press.

This has enabled us to correct a small number of errors which had occurred in that transcription, and occasionally to revert to Flora's phraseology and punctuation where we felt this was better than in the amended version.

We have also looked at a number of her earlier typescript drafts, some of which (including the 'new' chapter) were discovered in the last few years by Flora's biographer Gillian Lindsay, and this has allowed us to add information which the previous version did not contain—and the publisher's own historical research has provided notes into the people and places Flora would have known while she was in 'Heatherley' during the years 1898–1901.

Thanks are due to Anne Mallinson for the Introduction; to Hester Whittle for the illustrations at the start of chapters; to The Harry Ransom Humanities Research Center at The University of Texas, Austin, for loan of original material; to Oxford University Press for permission to republish; and to Elizabeth Swaffield, Flora's granddaughter, for copyright permission.

Contents

❧ ❧ ❧

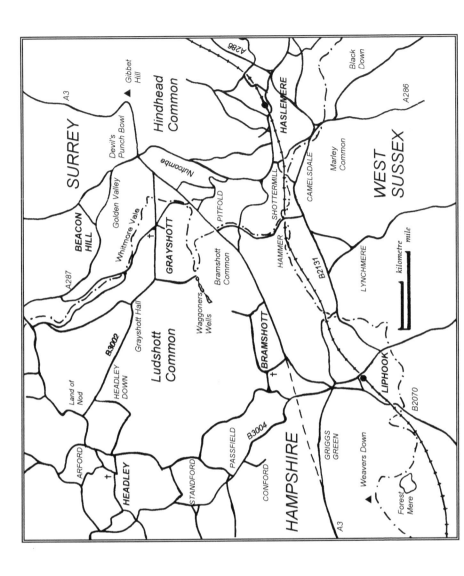

General map of the Grayshott, Haslemere, Headley and Liphook area

Introduction

Anniversaries often provide happy—and relevant—occasions for celebrations, and the publication of a new edition of *Heatherley* by Flora Thompson supplies the perfect opportunity to mark the centenary of the writer's arrival in Hampshire in the year 1898.

Flora Thompson, later to become the author of the captivating trilogy *Lark Rise to Candleford*, was twenty-one when she, in her own words, "walked without knowing it over the border into Hampshire ...", arriving in the village of Grayshott situated on the Surrey/Hampshire border—and the fictitious place name of 'Heatherley' was born.

Anyone who knows this Hampshire village which developed out of local heathlands in the 1860s will recognise the location at once. For, although Flora was a past-master at disguising the identities of both people and places in her prose, her descriptions were always accurate and clearly defined—to such an intriguing degree that the publisher of this book has already been sufficiently enthused to write his own journey *On the Trail of Flora Thompson* (1997) in which he sets out to discover their true identities.

I first became aware of Flora Thompson's *Heatherley* almost thirty years ago. And I owe a debt of gratitude to the late eminent biographer, Margaret Lane (1907–1994) for introducing me to this piece of writing—*and* for providing me with a pleasurable ongoing 'pursuit with a purpose.'

As Flora's first biographer—in the form of an original memoir published in the Spring number of *The Cornhill Magazine* in 1957, ten years after Flora's death—Margaret Lane's biographical essay was to open an unexpected literary 'door' into the Hampshire world of Flora Thompson. It was a tantalising account of her search into Flora's somewhat secretive life. Later the essay was included in *Purely for Pleasure*, a volume of Margaret Lane's literary and biographical essays. In 1976 it was republished, again by John Murray, to celebrate the centenary of Flora Thompson's birth.

In 1979 an extended version of the original memoir was published, with John Murray's approval, by Oxford University Press (OUP) as the Introduction to *A Country Calendar and other writings*. This was a volume of Flora Thompson's previously uncollected or unpublished papers which Margaret Lane had selected from material deposited at the University of Texas. And so *Heatherley*—which was included in the volume—was published ... at last!

* * *

By then, my own researches into the world of Flora Thompson had been under way for close on ten years.

In the autumn of 1970, after a busy year in Selborne commemorating the 250th anniversary of the birth of our famous naturalist and writer, Gilbert White, I had decided to take a break from my small, specialist, country bookshop—which I had founded two years previously and where the small companion volumes of White's *Natural History of Selborne* and Flora Thompson's *Lark Rise to Candleford*, in the 'World's Classics' edition, had already proved to be two of the most sought after books on my shelves.

Already familiar, of course, with White and his village of Selborne, I had a desire to find out more about the life of the author of *Lark Rise*, born in the hamlet amid the flat wheatfields of north east Oxfordshire almost a century before, in 1876.

There was no doubt that Juniper Hill *was* 'Lark Rise' of the books, and when I arrived there the larks were still singing above the stubble fields of another harvest gone—and 'The Fox' was there too, the village inn described by Flora as the 'Wagon and Horses'.

Over a sandwich and a sherry in this evocative place (alas, now closed as I write) the landlord, on hearing of my pilgrimage, passed a worn and well-thumbed typescript across the bar—it was Margaret Lane's biographical essay on Flora Thompson published in *The Cornhill* in 1957. I sat reading, fascinated—and sufficiently carried away with emotion, and excitement at my discovery of so much previously unknown information, that I ordered "the same again please" and read on.

The word 'Hampshire' and the names of Grayshott and Liphook sprang from the pages. Here, indeed, was a key to be turned ... and the Hampshire world of Flora Thompson to be discovered.

Early in 1973 I decided to bring Flora Thompson into a special display in my bookshop, and I wrote to Margaret Lane seeking her help with display material and information. "Alas," she wrote, "I have nothing of Flora Thompson's, not even an envelope. All the material, or nearly all of it, I got from her daughter, who is now dead [she died in 1966]. I have no idea where relics of Flora, if any, went"—and she referred me to a Mr A C Ward (a Reader at OUP) and suggested too that Miss Joan Hassall might just be able to help (Miss Hassall had illustrated Margaret Lane's essay in *The Cornhill*, and was herself a Flora Thompson devotee).

Sadly, Mr Ward in his reply had to admit that he too "did not keep the personal letters I had from her in the late 1940s", but mentioned the acquisition of her literary remains by the University of Texas, adding: "These included an unpublished typescript of a novel based largely on her post office experience, but alas! it hadn't anything of the immortal strain of the Lark Rise trilogy and I had to advise against publication."

However, Mr Ward kindly suggested that I wrote to Geoffrey Cumberlege, "sometime Publisher to the University of Oxford" — and from there on, my luck was in. Over a period of six years, until his death in 1979, Geoffrey Cumberlege encouraged and contributed towards my efforts to establish recognition of Flora Thompson in east Hampshire.

But to return to the story of *Heatherley* and the course of its journey towards publication. I wrote to Joan Hassall, whose name I knew well as an outstanding wood engraver and illustrator. She kindly replied by return of post, offering me photocopies of one or two of her items—a letter from Flora and extracts from a few letters from Winifred [Flora's daughter]—then going on to say: "The most interesting thing, if its whereabouts could be traced, would be the typescript which her daughter Winifred allowed me to read, of a fourth book of Laura's recollections founded on Flora's life at Grayshott. Vivian Ridler of OUP might know to whom Winifred left her mother's papers. OUP did not think the fourth book worth adding to the three, but to those who love Flora Thompson's work it was keenly interesting."

A further admirer of Flora, Miss Gertrude Oppenheimer, was also of the same opinion, and in 1976 she wrote to OUP suggesting an omnibus edition of Flora's selected unpublished writings.

OUP then wrote to Margaret Lane for her opinion as to "the feasibility, or indeed desirability of putting together such a volume," stating that "as well as the essays and stories there is *Heatherley* and *Bog Myrtle & Peat*", and a few days later I had a letter from her enclosing a copy of this and asking me to let her know what I thought. "I don't myself think," she wrote, "there would be any point in including much of the early unpublished work ... but *Heatherley* and *Bog Myrtle*, or extracts from them, might be a very good idea. Do you know where the material is at present?"

I replied with encouragement, and the proverbial ball began to roll. Numerous letters then passed between Margaret Lane and myself as I filled her in with the information she required and told her of the increasing interest I encountered in Flora's life and work. Further correspondence travelled between OUP and Margaret Lane's home in Beaulieu, and the project was set in motion.

In September 1976, she wrote to me: "We now hope to go ahead with a kind of omnibus-selection volume." The University of Texas provided photocopies of the material, and once again *Heatherley* crossed the Atlantic, home again for publication, and in the autumn of 1979, *A Country Calendar and other writings*— including *Heatherley*—was launched at The Selborne Bookshop.

I look back over the years of my involvement with Flora in east Hampshire: to the celebrations of the centenary of her birth in 1976 with the literary luncheon in Liphook; the unveiling in 1981 of the sculptured bust by Philip Jackson, now in Liphook library; and to the first Grayshott Literary Festival in 1995 when, on the opening evening, I spoke of Flora's link with the area, and actor David Wynn, well known in the locality, read passages from *Heatherley* and *The Peverel Papers*—Grayshott and Liphook in disguise.

Now it is a September again, and we await publication of this new edition of *Heatherley*, with its charming pen & ink illustrations and this introduction which it has given me much pleasure to record.

May it take its own place in the story of Flora's immortality— in the world which gave us her unique gifts, where her memory is now commemorated and cared for, and will not be forgotten.

Anne Mallinson
Selborne, September 1998

Laura goes farther

One hot September afternoon near the end of the last century[1] a girl of about twenty walked without knowing it over the border into Hampshire from one of its neighbouring counties. She was dressed in a brown woollen frock with a waist-length cape of the same material and a brown beaver hat decorated with two small ostrich tips, set upright in front, back to back, like a couple of notes of interrogation. This outfit, which would no doubt appear hideous to modern eyes,[2] had given her great moral support on her train journey. The skirt, cut short just to escape contact with the ground and so needing no holding up except in wet weather, was, her dressmaker had assured her, the latest idea for country wear. The hat she had bought on her way through London that morning. It had

---

[1] September 1898
[2] Written in about 1944

cost nine and eleven-pence three farthings of the pound she had saved to meet her expenses until her first month's salary was due in her new post, but she did not regret the extravagance for it became her brown eyes and hair and would help her, she hoped, to make a good impression at her journey's end. "A good first impression is half the battle", she had been told as a child, and she had special reasons for wishing to make a good impression today, for she had lately been somewhat unsettled through taking short holiday-relief engagements at the post offices where she had worked and this new position, she hoped, would prove a permanency. Her people at home were beginning to speak of her as a rolling stone, and rolling stones were not in favour with country people of that day. The plea that to work, even for a short time, in one of the larger post offices was a valuable gain in experience did not appeal to her parents. They looked upon experience as something to be gathered unconsciously, not a thing to be sought. They preferred permanence and security.

But Laura at that moment was not conscious of her appearance and had ceased to care about what impression she was likely to make. Even the uneasy fear that it was due to some mistake of her own that she had not been met, as promised, at the railway station had passed from her mind, for she had emerged from the deep, tree-shaded lane which led up from the little town in the dip,[3] come out upon open heath, and for the first time in her life saw heather growing. She recognised the flower immediately from a thousand descriptions she had read of it in its native haunts which she had supposed to be far north of the Thames, and from earliest childhood had carried with her a mental picture of the heatherclad hills and moors of Scott's novels and poems. Her preconceived idea seemed crude and cold before the living reality.

Pale purple as the bloom on a ripe plum, veined with the gold of late flowering gorse, set with small slender birches just turning yellow, with red-berried rowans and thickets of bracken, the heath lay steeped in sunshine. The dusty white road by which she had come was deserted by all but herself, and the only sounds to be heard were the murmuring of bees in the heathbells and the low, plaintive cries of a flock of linnets as they flitted from bush to bush. From where she stood she could see, far away on the horizon, a long wavy line of dim blue hills which to her, used as she was to a land of flat fields, appeared to be mountains. The air, charged with the

---

[3] Haslemere, Surrey

scent of heather and pine, had the sharp sweetness of wine and was strangely exhilarating to one accustomed from birth to the moist, heavy, pollen-laden air of the agricultural counties. She stood as long as she dared upon the edge of the heath, breathing long breaths and gazing upon the scene with the delight of a discoverer; then with a buoyant floating-upon-air feeling, passed on uphill towards the knot of red roofs which soon appeared among pine trees.

Heatherley,[4] as she afterwards found, was not strictly speaking a village at all, but a settlement of recent growth consisting of a couple of roads with shops, a new model inn with an artistic signboard and a few modern cottages and villas, many of them with an "Apartments to Let" card in the window. Since a famous scientist[5] had discovered the virtues of the moorland air and a Royal Academician had painted the scenery, the place had come into being to serve the convenience of those living in the large houses and staying at the hotels which had sprung up at every favourite viewpoint for miles around. There were other similar settlements in the district, but none of them, so far, had a telegraph office, so, though later it was to be superseded, Heatherley was and remained for a few years the chief postal centre.

Heatherley Post Office was a pretty red-tiled building with wide wooden eaves and a shop window which displayed choice leather goods such as writing and dressing-cases, bibles and prayer books, purses and photograph frames. In the doorway recess was a glass case of the new picture postcards with local views. Views were so far the only subject printed upon postcards; the portraits of musical comedy actresses, the collection of which was soon to become a craze, were as yet unthought of, and farther still in the future was the day of the coloured "comic". The modern note of advertisement, however, was already present, as shown by the caption, "The English Switzerland", beneath a view of some local hill scenery. The view was one of typical English moorland, beautiful on its own small scale but in no way challenging comparison with Alpine grandeur, and the name was probably due to a flight of fancy on the part of one of those out to exploit the place. In other circles the best-known hill near Heatherley was sometimes called the Lesser Parnassus because of the number of poets and other writers who haunted its slopes. But Laura, that afternoon, did not stay to look at the

---

[4] Grayshott, then in the parish of Headley
[5] John Tyndall, came to Hindhead 1883, died there 1893

pictured views or to read the captions. She opened the door timidly and made herself known.

As any kind of humble lodging was difficult to find it had been arranged that until she could find a room for herself in the village she should live with the postmaster's family; so she was taken at once to the living-room at the back of the office and handed over to the postmaster's wife. The room in which she found herself was of a type different from those of her recent experiences. This was no ordinary parlour behind a shop, with a sideboard display of silver, linoleum on the floor and framed photographs on the walls; but, as it appeared, the abode of people of some refinement. Yet as it seemed to Laura, if not at that time then later, there was something strange and gloomy, even a little sinister, about that room. The one window, perhaps because it was in a side wall and a path to the back premises ran beneath it, had been reinforced with a screen of painted glass which cast a dim, coloured light on the room. A huge, heavily carved oak cabinet, resembling in shape a Jacobean court cupboard, almost filled the wall on one side, and there was a good deal of other heavily carved oak furniture. This, she found later, had been made and carved by the postmaster, who was a cabinet-maker by trade and had a workshop somewhere at the back of the house. The walls of the room were plain-washed sage green and the only picture was a signed print of a painting by a local artist.

But Laura, though deeply interested, had no time then for more than a hasty glance round, for her attention was naturally given to the wife of her new employer. Mrs Hertford[6] was as unusual for her time and position in life as was her room. She was tall, thin and faded, with drooping shoulders, a very pale face, and smooth straight masses of dull yellow hair which she wore combed low over her ears. She was in a late stage of pregnancy and wore a long loose green frock with much embroidery about the shoulders. Her voice was melancholy and her movements were silent and slow. Laura thought her face the saddest she had ever seen.

Two children were present, one a small boy, very like his mother in looks and dressed in a little suit which might have been made from the same piece of material as her gown. He was well-mannered, but too silent and grave for his age, and Laura thought he had recently been crying. Both mother and boy looked rather like vegetables or flowers which had been kept in the dark, away from

---

[6] Mrs Emily Chapman, neé Revelle

the sun. The baby girl, who had just awakened from her afternoon nap, was a lovely child with cheeks the colour of a wild rose, dark eyes and a mop of fair curls. She was warm from her bed and full of life and laughter and when Laura took her on her knee she at once, without prompting, threw her arms round her neck and kissed her. Her charming welcome was reassuring to Laura, who felt an air of restraint in the room for which she could not account.

When Mrs Hertford heard that Laura had walked up from the railway station she seemed both surprised and distressed. Her husband, she said, had himself intended to drive down to meet her in their little governess-cart. Was Laura sure she had not seen the cart, a little brown turnout with a piebald pony? Laura said she was quite sure, and did not in the least mind not being met. She had left her trunk in the booking office and had thoroughly enjoyed the walk; would not have missed it for anything. Then the small boy, Cecil,[7] came back from the errand on which his mother had sent him and said Miffy, the pony, was out in the paddock and William had told him that Daddy had gone out after dinner, he did not know where, but he had not said anything about meeting the young lady, and Mrs Hertford said that in that case Daddy must have forgotten; he was very forgetful at times, and would Laura like to see her bedroom.

Afterwards, in the post office, Laura took over from the assistant whose place she was taking. Miss Smithers was a woman of forty who had at one time been employed in the Central Telegraph Office in London and had been invalided out of the service with a small pension after a nervous breakdown. Judging by her twitching features and strained, absent-minded expression she was on the eve of a second breakdown. She left Heatherley the next morning, duly driven to the station in the governess-cart by William, the odd-job man, but not before she had told Laura that the household she was leaving was far from a happy one. Mr and Mrs Hertford had what she described as terrific bust-ups. They had had one an hour or two before Laura's arrival, which accounted for her train not being met at the station and for the strained atmosphere she found on her arrival. "But don't ask me what it's all about," she added, "to me there's never seemed any sense or reason in their quarrels. I expect it's just that she doesn't know how to manage him; it's generally the wife's fault in such cases. But they're all right otherwise, rather superior for country people, and I don't suppose their rows will

---

[7] Walter Jnr—see Notes at end of book

affect you as they do me. I've got a sensitive nature myself. I'm funny that way."

Laura was to be what was called "in charge of the office". That is, she was, with the help of a junior assistant, to undertake all the postal and telegraph duties and make up the daily accounts which had then to be signed by the postmaster, who was responsible to the higher authorities. Beyond guaranteeing the efficient working of the office and the safe custody of the cash and other valuables, Mr Hertford[8] had little to do with the office. But he was no employer of sweated labour; the arrangement was known to and permitted by the authorities, and after he had paid the salaries of his assistants from his official income only a small margin was left to reward him for his responsibilities and to pay office rent. The post-office business was but a sideline to supplement his main income from working at his trade.

Laura's junior, Alma Stedman,[9] was a pretty, blue-eyed, sweet-natured girl of eighteen whose home was in the village. It was one of Laura's duties to teach Alma to manipulate the newly-installed single-needle telegraph instrument. This had been placed in a small passage, a mere cupboard with a window, between the public office and the living-room. It was worked by tapping out the letters of out-going telegrams in the Morse code and receiving incoming ones by watching, or reading by sound, according to the degree of efficiency of the operator, the single needle mounted on a green dial, which struck, now right, now left, upon two metal sounders. The striking needle made a pretty, musical tinkling sound which could be heard and interpreted, by those accustomed to it, at some distance from the instrument. Laura's life at Heatherley ran to the tune of its musical tinkling, and the mention or thought of the place in after years brought back its sound, that and the scent of heather and peat and pine, and in the background, the strife and unrest of lives which for a time impinged upon her own.

The old single-needle instrument has long disappeared from the post-office scene to make way for new labour-saving and easier-to-learn inventions. But at Heatherley in Laura's time it was regarded as a symbol of progress, and the mastery of its mysteries stamped the operator as thoroughly up to date and efficient. After Miss Smithers had departed no one in the village but Laura could work it,

---

[8] Walter Gillman Chapman, born at Barley, Hertfordshire
[9] Annie Symonds, born 29th Sept 1878 in Liscard, Cheshire

and until Alma became proficient her working hours were twelve daily, with no weekly half-day off and two hours' duty on Sunday morning. It had been agreed that as soon as Alma had qualified and could be left in charge of the instrument they should on alternate evenings finish work at six.

Shortly before the office closed on the evening of Laura's arrival Mr Hertford appeared. She had not heard him come into the office, for he wore soft-soled shoes which made no sound, and she turned round suddenly to find him standing behind her, laughing silently at her start of surprise. He was a dark, slightly-built man of forty-five who might have been thought handsome but for the peculiar tint of his complexion, which was a deep, dull mauvish-leaden shade, and the strange wild light in his eyes. The silent laughter was a habit of his. He was of a serious, somewhat gloomy nature and seldom smiled, but when anything appealed to his peculiar sense of humour he would throw back his head and go through a pantomime of hilarious laughter without uttering a sound. Another disquieting habit of his was that of quoting texts of scripture or lines from the poets in a hissing whisper. "Vengeance is mine ..." or "To be or not to be ..." he would hiss under his breath, *à propos* of nothing that had gone before, when taking up the pen to sign the accounts, or even at the family meal table.

But in spite of these and many other peculiarities, Laura in many ways liked Mr Hertford. That evening he welcomed her cordially, and he was reasonable in his business relations and an expert at his trade. During the time Laura knew him he did a good business in making articles of furniture which his customers of artistic taste designed for their own homes. He also carved and fitted the woodwork of a private chapel in the house of a Catholic resident, built and fitted with bookshelves a summerhouse for a poet's outdoor study, and framed pictures for an exhibitor at the Royal Academy. He took no part in local affairs and seldom came in contact with ordinary post-office customers, many of whom were under the impression that Laura was postmistress and addressed her as such. But he had a small space at the post-office counter reserved for his intercourse with his own trade customers, and it was evident from the nature of his interviews there that they had a high opinion of his talents and taste. An exhibitor, for instance, to comply with the regulations had to have his black and white drawings framed in gilt, which frames, he remarked, would be of no earthly use afterwards. Mr Hertford suggested that ebony frames should be lightly gilded and afterwards sandpapered back to the natural colour of the wood. At such interviews there was no hissing of texts or silent laughter; his was the quiet, helpful, deferential but not too deferential manner of a master craftsman discussing work with a customer.

He had read widely and seen something of the world. In his early twenties he had spent some years in Australia and on his voyages to and from that continent he had taken the opportunity of exploring the Mediterranean ports where passengers were permitted to land. He was a master of debate and to hear him and his brother,[10] who lived near, discuss politics and theology was a revelation to one who had gained such little knowledge as she possessed from the printed word. At such times his face would light up with enthusiasm and his ordinary habit of speech would give place to the clear, ringing tones of conviction.

His brother was a nonconformist in religion, a devoted chapel-goer; Mr Hertford attended neither church nor chapel and, as far as could be gathered from his ordinary conversation, was a sceptic; yet in these debates he would contend hotly for an established Church with a priesthood and bishops and archbishops, while his brother was all for self-government by the congregation. Words such as "sacerdotalism" and "hierarchical" flew to and fro between them and feeling often rose to such a point that the brother would rise and leave the house without saying goodnight; but always at their next meeting they were at it again.

During these discussions Mrs Hertford would sit silent in a low chair by the hearth, her pale hair drooping rather untidily over her sewing. She was glad to see her husband interested and occupied, but she herself cared nothing for such subjects. Her passion was music, and in her rare hours of domestic peace she would sing or hum airs from the operas or speak, of the days before her marriage when she had heard such and such a famous singer or pianist, or tell of the musical evenings at the house where she had been nursery governess and her services as an accompanist had been much in request. Musically, she had to live on such memories, for she had no piano of her own and only once during the time Laura knew her did she go out to hear music.

That was when a series of concerts of chamber music was given at a newly-built hall in the next settlement and, as tickets were sold

---

[10] Ernest Henry Chapman

and a plan of the hall was kept at the post office, a two-guinea ticket for the series was sent to the postmaster as an acknowledgement of the service.

Mrs Hertford so seldom left the house, even for an hour, that her going caused quite a flutter of excitement in the establishment. Alma had volunteered to mind the children and get tea ready and, without help, Laura would be especially busy in the post office. Mrs Hertford dressed with care and looked well in black with touches of yellow, her pale hair framed in a black lace hat with bunches of artificial cowslips. All except her husband stood at the window or door to see her off, Alma holding up the new baby. Its mother looked quite happy and cheerful when she turned to smile and wave back to them at the street corner. She returned in a state of exaltation, full of the music she had heard and especially of Miss Fanny Davies's piano playing; but that very evening her husband had one of his wildest outbursts of temper and she went to bed weeping. For the rest of the series of concerts the post-office ticket was unused.

Laura never heard the beginning of one of these domestic upheavals, and for some time their cause, real or imaginary, was a mystery to her. At one meal-time all would be peaceful, then, before the next became due, working quietly at the telegraph instrument where she could not help hearing most of what passed in the living-room, she would suddenly become aware of a deep hissing of abuse on one side and heartbroken weeping on the other. When her husband would permit it, Mrs Hertford was almost slavishly subservient towards him, and after his terrible outbreaks had subsided appeared to feel no resentment, only a pathetic desire to make peace. And a brittle, fugitive peace would be made between them, though it seldom lasted more than a week or two. As the weeks passed Laura became quite accustomed to going indoors for a meal and finding no cloth on the table, Mr Hertford glooming alone by the fireside and his wife and children locked in their bedroom upstairs. Afterwards, for several days, Mr and Mrs Hertford would not communicate with each other directly at table but addressed the remarks intended for each other to Laura, with whom, throughout, both husband and wife remained on ordinary terms. Every few weeks a new small maid would appear, to help Mrs Hertford with the housework and children, but none of these stayed longer than a month, some but a day or two. After one of Mr Hertford's outbursts the girl's mother would appear, declaring she was not going to have her child frightened to death by *their* quarrels, and depart with her daughter's belongings in a bundle under one arm and the hand of the other holding that of her daughter, who was usually crying.

The one person who helped to make tolerable those early days of Laura's life at Heatherley was her junior in the office, Alma Stedman. She was a short, rather sturdily built girl with pretty nut-brown hair and big blue eyes. "The little blue-eyed girl" was the description applied to her by strangers who wished to speak of her but did not know her name. Although in looks a typical country girl, hers was no common nature. Good and sincere, untouched by the world and its problems and yet no fool, with inborn good taste and a sense of humour, she was one of those rare persons who are happy and contented and wish for no change in their lives. The tempestuous life of the Hertfords affected her less than it did Laura. For one thing she saw and heard less of it, and for another she refused to believe it was caused by anything more than incompatibility of temperament. Married couples, she maintained, were prone to such fallings-out and fallings-in, and Laura, although unconvinced that the Hertford upheavals were mere ordinary married tiffs, for the time being felt reassured and comforted.

But what Laura liked best about Alma was that she was a reader, and especially fond of poetry. Not so much the work of the great poets or that of the more robust type of lesser poet, as smaller, more exquisite things with a touch of magic or faery about them. *Goblin Market, The Forsaken Merman* and Keats's *La Belle Dame Sans Merci* she knew by heart. Christina Rossetti was Alma's favourite poet and it was from her Laura first heard of the work of Coventry Patmore. Alma's taste in everything ran to the small and exquisite. The violet and the snowdrop were her favourite flowers, and, as a view, she preferred some mossy nook with primroses blooming against tree boles to the wide, purple expanse of the heath in its glory. They would sometimes contend a little over their preferences and Laura once wrote a little poem[11] for her, beginning:

You talk of pale primroses, of fair and fragrant posies,
The cowslip and the cuckoo-flower that scent the spring-time lea,
    But give to me the heather,
    The honey-scented heather,
    The glowing gypsy heather,
That is the flower for me!

---

[11] Later published by her in *Bog Myrtle and Peat*, 1921

Although Alma's good taste was inborn it had not gone uncultivated. She had not had to make her own discoveries in literature, as Laura had done. Her father was a gardener and the lady by whom he was employed held a Sunday afternoon class, or poetry reading, for a few selected girls of whom Alma was one. It also included the lady's two nieces, her parlourmaid, the bookkeeper at the steam laundry, and a pupil teacher at the village school. Every week Mrs Camden[12] read a poem of her own selection and commented upon its points of beauty and interest and the girls were then expected to learn it by heart and to repeat it to her on the following Sunday. By this means she hoped to form their taste and certainly in Alma's case her plan had worked very well. The only drawback to the plan that Laura could see was that it rather limited the range of her pupil. What Mrs Camden liked Alma liked so much that she was not inclined to venture further, certainly not to trust her own taste and judgement. She had the advantage of knowing on good authority what books and poems were worthy of her love, but she missed such thrills as Laura experienced when, having come casually upon some book or poem and loving it, she afterwards learned that it was an acknowledged masterpiece.

Alma's was a bright, sunshiny nature. The sorrows, injustices and inequalities of human life did not loom like a dark cloud on her horizon. When any special instance of sorrow or suffering came to her notice she would grieve sincerely and do all in her power to help or comfort those affected, but every such case was to her an isolated case, not a sign that all was not well with the world. Laura, on the other hand, was, as people told her, too much inclined to look on the dark side of life. Those were the days of the Boer War and she could not help picturing to herself as scenes of suffering those battlefields which, to those around her, were so many steps to final victory, or grieving for the ruined homesteads of the enemy and pitying the Boer women in the concentration camps, mourning their dead or in a state of anxiety for their living, just as the women in this country were mourning or anxious. She was anxious herself about her brother who was out there with his regiment, especially when month after month passed without her or any of her family receiving a letter from him.

When Alma saw her doing what she called "brooding" she had pretty, innocent ways of trying to cheer her which, though often

---

[12] Mrs Bulley of Westdown, Hindhead

simple to silliness, would usually raise a smile. Sorting the night mail, she would read out the addresses on the letters, pronouncing the place names grotesquely—Swanage ... Swanaggie, Metropole ... Met-ropoly, Leicester ... Ly-ces-ter, and so on. She would hide Laura's one ring, taken off for hand-washing, or shut up the office cat in the registered letter locker and pretend it was a tiger behind the wire netting. One day she brought a dead bee on her palm and presented it gravely to Laura, saying, "Is this not a bee you have lost from your bonnet?"

For some time after Laura first knew Alma she hoped she had found what she had not yet had, a close friend of her own age and sex. But no close friendship developed. Alma, living in the village, had her own home interests and friends of long standing; she was also spending much of her off-duty time with the young man she afterwards married, and her life was already full. They remained as they had begun, upon friendly terms, and looking back in after years, Laura felt that she owed much to her sweet, wholesome influence.

But even with Alma's companionship for many hours of each day and that of the new friends she was making, hers was an uncomfortable position and, when week after week passed with no early prospect of finding a room for herself in the village, she was often on the verge of giving notice to leave her post and seeking a more peaceful life elsewhere. But she was indoors sharing the Hertfords' life but a very few hours each day. With her work in the office she was perfectly satisfied, for she liked the bustle and stimulus of having plenty to do, the new public was interesting, and in her off-duty daylight hours she had a new and enthralling country to explore. Moreover she had no money with which to meet removal expenses. Her mother, she knew, would have managed somehow to provide that had she been told of the circumstances, but it would have been at great self-sacrifice, and although she had other relatives who would willingly have helped her, such a horror of borrowing had been instilled into her mind from earliest childhood that she never once thought of applying to them.

So she stayed on at Heatherley and gathered there much experience, both pleasant and unpleasant. "Foolish nineteen and wicked one-and-twenty" was an old saying of the countryside of her birth. A modern author has called the same period in human life Sinister Street. Laura's Sinister Street was, after all, not so very sinister, but, such as it was, she had to pass through it and fate had decreed that that passing through should take place at Heatherley.

The Villagers

In her early days at Heatherley, Laura sometimes felt that she had strayed into a new world. A more prosperous and leisured, a more sophisticated, and on many subjects a better informed, but a less kindly, solid, and permanent world than that of her birth. That impression may have been due partly to the coming and going of visitors in holiday mood, and because, in that new district, few who lived there had been born in the place or had lived there as children. Some of the shopkeepers, married men with families, still spoke of Birmingham, London, or Shropshire as home. Both the Heatherley doctors were new to the village, as was the clergyman, for the church was but newly built.[13] Nearly all the working people had come there simply to earn a livelihood, as indeed had Laura herself.

[13] St Luke's, Grayshott, built 1898–1900

None of these had had time to get rooted in the soil, even if they had had the inclination.

But not all that went to make up the impression was due to locality. The times were changing and people were changing with the times. Of this change Laura had missed several stages. In agricultural counties, such as that of her birth, people were still much as they had been in her childhood. Those born on the land, with very few exceptions, lived and died on the land. New ideas were long in reaching them and were seldom received kindly when they arrived. The old family names survived generation after generation in the villages, and the very fields with their customary rotation of crops helped to confirm the feeling of continuity.

The Heatherley villagers, having broken with their own personal past and come to a place without traditions, appeared to live chiefly for the passing moment. The past, especially the country past, was nothing to them, and if they looked forward to a future it was a future of change, to the comfort and ease of a well-earned retirement for themselves and, more vaguely, for the world at large; and to the good time which newspaper prophets assured them was to come with the new century, when new machinery would be invented to do the work and man, with unlimited leisure, would live on a tabloid diet at the cost of a penny a day.

In the meantime new fashions in dress and ways of living, new arrivals in the district with money to spend, new items of local gossip and new ideas culled from the day's newspaper—new today and forgotten tomorrow—were, outside their own family affairs, their main preoccupation. Fundamentally they were much as mankind has always been. They had their hopes and fears, likes and dislikes, they worked hard at their trade, or serving in their shops, or waiting upon the sojourners in their apartments, bearing their troubles and reverses more or less bravely, sacrificing themselves for those they loved or accepting the sacrifice of others, for though manners and ideas may change, human nature is changeless.

Manners and customs were certainly changing. The Heatherley shopkeepers were more independent in their manner towards their customers than the old style village tradesmen, cultivating the take-it-or-leave-it manner which they thought became a free-born Briton. Their shops were smaller and not so well kept as those in the small towns and villages of Laura's childhood and they had not the pride in the quality of their goods and their own ability to oblige which had marked the old-fashioned butcher or grocer. Many of the richer residents had their provisions sent weekly from Whiteley's or the Army and Navy Stores, and some of the poorer combined business and pleasure by Saturday night shopping in the nearest town. Neither rich nor poor felt any moral obligation to deal with local shops. They made their purchases where they thought the goods were likely to be fresher or cheaper.

There was a similar loosening of other relations. The lord of the manor, for instance, who being untitled would in a village of the older type have been known as the Squire and reigned more or less beneficently over his small kingdom, was to the Heatherley villagers simply Mr Doddington[14] who lived in such-and-such a large house. He exercised no particular influence upon the villagers, who respected him just as much and no more than any other rich local man who paid his bills regularly. Between his periods of foreign travel he entertained such neighbours as were generally considered his equals, but did not pretend to know everyone in the village or feel it his duty to enquire as to the health and well-being of those who were known to him. He was said to be a good employer to those who worked on his estate and to be kind to them and their families in trouble or sickness, but such kindness, together with his other charities, if he were charitably inclined, were unofficial. He lived the life of a private gentleman, as did the other score or so of private gentlemen living in the neighbourhood, being neither the petty tyrant nor the kindly patron known in less up-to-date parishes as Our Squire.

Between doctor and patient there must always be to some degree a personal relationship, but although both the Heatherley doctors were well liked and their skill respected, the relationship existing between them and their ordinary village patients was not that of the old country doctor and patient. In Laura's childhood, she well remembered, there was in most instances a tie of close affection and, on the one side, of gratitude. An ordinary countrywoman with little of her own in store would when going to the market town to pay her doctor's bill—or more often a small instalment of it—carry with her some little offering, mushrooms, a rabbit, a bottle of home-made wine or ketchup, saying, "I know 't isn't much and he's got plenty, but I feel that no money can ever pay for what he done for our so-and-so." In the newer order money was considered a suffi-

---

[14] Presumably Mr Alexander Ingham Whitaker of Grayshott Hall—there was no lord of the manor as such

cient payment. People received much larger doctor's bills and paid them more or less promptly with no more than the ordinary amount of grumbling, and the obligation was considered cancelled.

At Heatherley the cottages and villas interspersed with the shops were occupied by gardeners, coachmen and other outdoor workers at the larger houses, by the families of men who worked at their different trades for the local builder, and by widows and maiden ladies who let apartments. There were no really poor people and few who could be called "country people" in the ordinary sense of the term. To find those native to the place one had to go outside the village. There, tucked away in the long narrow valleys of the heath, were small ancient homesteads, each with its two or three fields, where the descendants of the original inhabitants of the countryside farmed on the smallest possible scale, exercised to the full their commoners' rights and sold butter and eggs and garden produce to the newcomers. They also carried on the old local industry of making the small, round garden brooms called besoms from the long, tough stems of the heather and on that account were still spoken of by the old traditional name of broom-squires.

Laura, on her rambles, was later to see something of the broom-squires' little low houses with ricks built of the few handfuls of hay from their fields and other much larger and taller piles, built rick-wise, of new heather brooms with shining white, newly-peeled handles, ready to be taken to market; but when she had first arrived at Heatherley her immediate interest was centred on the celebrities. There were at that time far more of these than of the broom-squires. The widow of the famous scientist who had discovered the place was still living in the house he had built and afterwards fenced on one side with a fifteen-foot screen thatched with heather to hide from view the new houses built by others who had profited by his discovery. A judge who was also a man of letters had a weekend cottage there, an African explorer who had recently been in the forefront of the news had taken a furnished house, and a young publisher whose name was later to be familiar to all readers was a frequent visitor. There were many writers and artists, both well-known and lesser-known, and just at that time it was the writers who were supposed to confer its special distinction on the locality.

On her first Sunday morning walk Laura had seen a tall man on a crutch, with a forked red beard and quick, searching eyes, surrounded by a group of younger men who appeared to be drinking in his every syllable. The tall man with the crutch, she was told, was a writer.[15] He had but recently come there and no-one quite knew what he wrote, but it was known that he was thought a lot of in London. Very clever, they said, very clever indeed. The followers were young men from town who, since he had injured his leg in a cycling accident, came at weekends to visit him. Laura had been a voracious reader from early childhood; most of her adventures so far had been among books, and to see a living author was as exciting to her as a good view of a living film star would be to many girls of today. She was to see that particular author again, many times, and to listen with delight to his conversation with friends he met at the post-office counter. Other authors, too, many of whose names and writings were already familiar to her.

One writer especially,[16] who had invented a new type of fiction which is still flourishing at the present day, though the author has, as he himself would express it, long "passed over". His was the kind of book which appeals to everybody young and old, intellectual and simple, and he had then recently scored a big success which had made a great impression on the villagers; not so much by his litera-ture as by the big fancy-dress ball he had given at the new hotel on the hill to celebrate it. Scarcely a day passed without his bursting like a breeze into the post office, almost filling it with his fine presence and the deep tones of his jovial voice. As he went about the village he had a kindly greeting for all, rich and poor, known and unknown alike. He was probably the most popular man in the neighbourhood. Practically everyone had read at least one of his books and many of his local readers fully believed him to be the greatest of living authors.

Another resident, also a novelist,[17] though a novelist of a dif-ferent type, had just caused a sensation by publishing one of the new "problem" novels which were a feature of the nineties. It was a serious book written by an acknowledged master of style and the situation it dealt with and the method of treatment would appear legitimate and restrained to the novel-reader of today. But then it raised a storm of criticism of its supposed loose morals. Letters were written to the newspapers about it, sermons were preached against it and it was banned by some of the libraries. Everybody who knew the author by sight, or even the outside of the house he

---

[15] George Bernard Shaw, then in his 40s and recently married

[16] Arthur Conan Doyle, who had recently built *Undershaw* at Hindhead

[17] Grant Allen, died 25th October 1899

lived in, felt a burning desire to read his book and copies were bought and handed round until practically everyone of mature age in the village had read and passed judgement on it. The first reaction to it was shocked but delighted excitement. Whoever'd have thought that that quiet-looking little gentleman with the neat grey beard and the field-glasses slung over his shoulder could think up and write down in black and white such a shocking tale. And would he be prosecuted for writing it? They had heard of Court cases over improper books, and some who had secretly enjoyed reading his novel seemed quite disappointed when the pother it had caused died down and the author still walked at large, apparently unperturbed by the storm he had raised.

Another frequent visitor at the post office was a young poet[18] whose work was then held in high esteem in literary circles. In those days poets still dressed the part. Only a few years before, not many miles from Heatherley, Tennyson[19] himself might have been seen, a noble figure in his black cloak and wide slouch hat, pacing the heath and murmuring aloud to himself the lines he was then fashioning. George Macdonald, in a bath chair, his beautiful white hair set off by a scarlet coat, had been a familiar sight in the streets of the little town in the valley. Theirs had been revered figures in which the whole neighbourhood felt an almost proprietary interest; but the new young poet, who actually lived at Heatherley, was little regarded locally.

He should have attracted more attention, for he raced about the parish at all hours on his bicycle with his halo of long, fair hair uncovered and his almost feminine slightness and grace set off by a white silk shirt, big artist's bow tie and velvet knickerbockers. But he was young. His portrait did not appear in the newspapers on his birthday with a caption claiming him as a national asset, and his works, bound in velvet yapp, were not available for Christmas and birthday gifts. For the commonalty he did not as yet exist.

These and many other well-known people came to the post-office and Laura had her restricted post-office-counter view of them all. Some of them were brilliant conversationalists and when two or more friends or neighbours met there it amused her to listen to their talk. She would sometimes wish that one of those quick, clever remarks they tossed like coloured glass balls into the air could have

---

[18] Richard Le Gallienne
[19] Tennyson died at Aldworth, near Haslemere, in 1892

come her way, for in her youthful vanity she persuaded herself that she could have caught and returned it more neatly than someone to whom it was addressed. In her business relations with them she found as a general rule that those ranking high intellectually, like those of high social rank, were easy and pleasant to deal with. It was those with but some small success to their credit and those who were socially ambitious but of insecure social position that she found self-important and patronising.

Then there were the Bohemian hangers-on of literature and the arts who, while the place was fashionable, would come, knapsack on shoulder, and put up at a public or an apartment house. A familiar figure for some time in the village was a young man who had taken a room at a public house and given out that he had come there to write a novel. He was a tall lanky creature who in his black Inverness cloak and soft slouch hat resembled a down-and-out Bohemian artist as seen in a *Punch* drawing. To obtain local colour, as he himself would have expressed it, he associated with the one bad character in the neighbourhood, a permanently out of work ne'er-do-well of about his own age who was suspected of poaching and known to be a foul-mouthed blackguard.

The better-class residents had nothing to do with him, though on account of his peculiar appearance everybody in the village must have known him by sight. To the ordinary villagers he was a figure of fun to be laughed at and winked over. One of Laura's most painful memories was that of seeing him one evening of rejoicing for a Boer War victory, half drunken and with a girl of about fourteen on his arm. The girl was looking up into his flushed, foolish-looking face with adoring eyes as she guided his unsteady feet towards the inn where he lodged. Perhaps it was well for her that not many days later he was found dead by his own hand with only a few coppers in his possession and deeply in debt to his landlord.

His death made a great impression on the villagers. People were horrified, not so much by the squandering of a young life as because the dance in the assembly room above his bedroom, already arranged for the night after his death, was not postponed. The dance took place. In the room above all was laughter and gaiety, in the room beneath lay the lifeless remains of one whose life, who knows how hopefully begun, had come to nothing.

Laura saw a sad little sequel. A respectable-looking elderly man, a clerk, perhaps, or a small shopkeeper, who was apparently the dead youth's father, came the next day to attend the inquest and arrange the funeral. He came to the post office to send off some telegrams and Laura could not help noticing that, as he stood aside writing them, his tears were dropping on to the telegraph forms and on to his neatly rolled umbrella.

A very different character was the grave, earnest, spectacled young man who, for a whole summer, occupied a room at the house of one of the broom-squires. He had come there in the first place to recuperate after an illness, but he too had literary ambitions and was writing a novel. When he called at the post office during a quiet spell he would stay talking to Laura about books, quoting long passages and asking if she preferred this or that, which was flattering to her taste, though it must be confessed that he seldom waited for her answer. Once, while sheltering at the post office from a heavy shower which kept everyone else indoors, he told her about the novel he was writing. He had come to a difficult place, he said, and would like her advice. In accordance with his prearranged plot he had now to describe a suicide. The whole story turned on that, but his conscience was troubled lest some future reader should be influenced by the example of his character.

He was so tied to the one idea and yet so distressed about it and he took his future reader so much for granted that his genuine scruple seemed funny to Laura, and she treated the matter so lightly that he was offended. Their budding friendship was nipped for ever. But not before he had done her the great service of introducing her to the work of George Meredith, of which she soon became so great an admirer that she could have passed a stiffish examination in the plots and characters of his novels and could, had she had a listener, have quoted most of his simpler poems. His novels revealed a new world to her, a world where women existed in their own right and not merely, whether loved or unloved, as the complement of man. Diana of the Crossways, Lucy Feverel, Sandra Belloni, Rose Josceline, and dearest of all "that dainty rogue in porcelain", Clara Middleton, she loved them all and rejoiced in their fine gallant spirit and brilliant wit. She accepted the author's word that there were such women, though she had herself never come in contact with any woman half as delightful, and thought of their world as a paradise of the well-born and well-educated, from which she was barred by her birth.

In time her first fervour subsided, the bright vision of Meredith's world receded into the background of her consciousness, a permanent possession but no longer paramount, and her incense was burnt before other shrines, as is the way of youth. While the fever of enthusiasm was at its height she went one summer Sunday to Box Hill to look upon the outside of Flint Cottage. She had not the good fortune to catch a glimpse of her idol. By that time Meredith was old and had become an invalid, and was probably at that hour taking his afternoon rest. But she had the satisfaction of beholding his abode and the view he looked out upon from his windows, with the added enjoyment of exploring Box Hill. Avoiding the many pairs of lovers ensconced in the lower nooks, she climbed to the summit and sat there enthroned to eat her buns and drink the medicine bottle of milk she had brought in the Dorothy bag swinging by long cords from her arm. Then a long, hot walk back to Mickleham station, not unmolested by the proffered attentions of trippers who, as a class, were far more unmannerly in those days than now, and another long trudge after her train journey; then to bed, very tired but blissfully content with her pious pilgrimage.

Meredith's novels and scores of other then modern books were obtained from the library shelves in a shop which stood across the road from the post office. *Madam Lillywhite, Milliner and Costumier, Baby Linen and Real Lace, Lending Library (frequent boxes from Mudie's), Stationery and Artists' Materials* ran the lettering above the door and in white enamel letters on the two windows. Madam Lillywhite[20] was a small, elderly, daintily dressed lady who must have had a passion for her stock of real lace, for she was always adorned with collars, cuffs, jabots and other furbelows of that delicate material. Over her picturesquely dressed grey hair she wore draped a lace shawl in the style of a Spanish mantilla, a mode of her own which did not however appear as freakish as might now be supposed in those days when many elderly ladies still wore some kind of lace headgear indoors. She did a thriving business with visitors to the place and employed several assistants including at one time a swarthy young man of Indian birth. Madam herself seldom appeared in the shop except to display her treasures of real lace to select customers. Her fellow tradesmen thought her odd, decidedly odd, and they did not like oddness. Above all they resented her styling herself Madam. She did not appear to care in the least for their good or bad opinion, but went her way, doing a good trade with the type of resident and visitor she had no doubt had in mind when establishing her business. Once a month she took train to

---

[20] 'Madame' Fanny Warr

London and returned with a small selection of fashionable and expensive hats and other goods, many of the things bought on commission for some individual customer. She was indeed a pioneer among the keepers of the exclusive little hat and frock shops we now see everywhere.

Laura could not afford to buy her clothes there, but by means of Madam's shelves and Mr Mudie's boxes she soon got in touch with current literature. There were poems and plays, as well as novels, and copies of such periodicals as the *Athenaeum, Nineteenth Century* and *Quarterly Review,* back numbers of which could be borrowed for a penny. Laura almost "read her head off", as her mother would have said, getting through everything she borrowed so quickly that she was often ashamed to return a book so soon, but driven on by an unquenchable thirst for novelty.

Sometimes she heard callers at the post-office counter discussing some new book she had read and it interested her to hear their opinion of it and compare it with her own. Literary people at that time, she found, were not enthusiastic about each others' books unless the author happened to be one of their own circle of friends. Kipling, for instance, then at the height of his reputation and much in the news, was not a general favourite in the colony. At the most his work received but faint praise. Laura heard one lady say that at home she and her husband always spoke of him as "The Big Noise", and another announced proudly that a certain writer whom she named had in an article criticised his work severely. Time proves all things, and the best of Kipling's work stands firm while the writer of the article has, as an authority, been long forgotten.

Such conversations were diverting when Laura had leisure and peace of mind to enjoy them, but more often than not she had neither. Her work kept her fairly busy, especially during the summer months, and there were worrying difficulties in the course of it. Most worrying of all was the difficulty of getting the telegrams for local delivery out promptly. Five telegraph messengers were employed in the summer, three in the winter, and in theory these were more than sufficient to deliver forty to fifty incoming telegrams at the height of the season. But in practice it was not so. The distance covered by the delivery was so great and the houses so widely scattered that there was often unavoidable delay. No sooner had Messenger No. 5 disappeared on his bicycle than another telegram would come for the very address to which he had gone, or for another near it, and that had to wait until Messenger No. 1

returned. The post office rules authorised the employment of casual messengers in such emergencies but no casual messenger was ever to be found, the villagers were all busy with their own more profitable affairs. This local condition the post office authorities could not or would not grasp and often correspondence about a delayed telegram clouded Laura's outlook for days.

One such ever-growing sheaf of papers went to and fro, from London to the local head office, from the head office to Heatherley, and from Heatherley to the head office and back to London, for weeks, and Laura was properly put in her place before the incident closed. It all began by a telegram for delivery arriving during a terrific thunderstorm. The older inhabitants of the place declared that they had never known such a thunderstorm. The thunder was deafening, the lightning terrible to behold, and these were followed by a deluge of rain. A cow was struck dead in a field at the back of the post office, this tragedy being reported by a small messenger boy who came in from his last delivery soaked to the skin and trembling with fear. Laura made a special journey to the postmaster's workshop to consult him as to whether or not the boy should be sent out again in such weather and in his condition, and they agreed that it would be unreasonable to expect him to go and that neither the authorities nor the person to whom the telegram was addressed would wish him to go until the storm abated. Accordingly, Laura sent the boy home to change his wet clothes and wrote upon the back of the telegram as the required explanation of the delay, "Severe thunderstorm raging".

Back from Headquarters came the telegram with her endorsement, a stiff letter of complaint about the delay from the addressee, and an official inquiry "as to the circumstances in which climatic conditions were taken into account". When writing the "further explanation" demanded, Laura dwelt upon the unusual severity of the thunderstorm, the condition and age of the messenger boy, and introduced the dead cow as evidence. But if she expected the official mind to be open to such reasoning she was disappointed. "Climatic conditions", she was told in the next missive, "are no excuse for the non-delivery of a telegram when a messenger is available. Your reply to No. 18, such-and-such a date, is highly unsatisfactory. You will now return these papers with the telegram properly endorsed and an undertaking that no similar incident occurs in future", and Laura, greatly daring, undertook as directed the control of the elements by writing, "Error regretted. Care shall be taken that it does not occur again", which meaningless formula apparently gave full satisfaction, for she heard no more of the matter.

At that time the telephone system did not extend to country places and the telegraph was the only quick and ready means of communication. People used it for purposes for which they would now "ring up"—to send invitations to friends living near them, to enquire as to the progress of invalids, and to give orders to trades-men. Then telegrams of almost letter length, not at all urgent in appearance, were sent by rich or impulsive people. Some of these last were love letters and many a promising affair took shape and was brought to a happy or a disastrous conclusion through Laura's mediumship.

One outstanding instance may serve to show the almost unbelievable distance we have travelled in the matter of communi-cation since those pre-telephone and pre-motor-car days. A so-far childless couple living in a large country house near Heatherley were looking forward to what was then called "an interesting event". They were rich, the lady was not strong in health, their long-deferred hope was about to be fulfilled, and they naturally spared no expense in their arrangements. The first intimation of the expected event at the post office was that for a week, beginning on a stated date a few months ahead, a day and night telegraph service must be arranged. This, as afterwards transpired, was in order that a London specialist could be summoned by telegraph at any hour, day or night. If after midnight, it had been arranged that he should travel by special train from Waterloo.

As it turned out, the well-thought-out programme proved un-necessary, for the baby (good, sensible child) decided to make its appearance at an hour when the telegraph was working and trains were running normally; but that such a programme was pre-arranged, not for the birth of a royal prince or princess but for the child of a plain country gentleman, gives some idea of the great change made in country life by those comparatively new amenities, the telephone and the motor car. Now, of course, in such circum-stances when the hour approached, the patient would either be already in a nursing home or her husband would quickly convey her to one in their own car. Or if, having every comfort and convenience around her, she preferred to remain in her own home, the telephone would soon summon the requisite attendance.

The poorer invalids when they had to be taken to hospital had no smooth, silent-running motor ambulance to convey them. They travelled, often in a sitting position, in whatever horsed vehicle happened to be available. There were no motor buses to take people for pleasure trips or to do their shopping in the nearest town. At Heatherley there were not even horse buses. The poorer went on foot, the richer in their own private turnout, carriage, dog-cart, or governess-cart.

The country roads were not as yet tar-surfaced but left to their natural dust or muddiness. In summer, in dry weather, every vehicle which passed over them moved in a thick cloud of white dust. But no one seemed to notice that or to feel any discomfort. They congratulated themselves on having what they considered good, modern, made-up roads, instead of the former cart-tracks.

By the end of the century, in such modernised parts of the country as the Heatherley district, there was little class consciousness. Except in remote rural villages, the time had gone when every member of the community knew his or her own place in the social system and their places were exactly defined. Laura could remember hearing the witty old postmistress under whom she had served her apprenticeship lay down a ruling in that respect. A retired tailor from a town who had been but a year or two in the village had been invited to the great house to inspect the squire's collection of coins, in which he had expressed interest. "But it's such a tremendous place," he told Miss Lane, "I've been wondering all the morning which door I ought to go to." Miss Lane looked him up and down appraisingly, kept silence for a moment, then asked, "Does Squire send you pheasants or rabbits at Christmas?" "Oh, rabbits," said the man, looking rather surprised at the question, "and I think it's very good of him, being as I am a newcomer." "Then," said the postmistress judicially, "it's the side door you should go to." A gift of game, it appeared, implied social, if not financial equality, and such a gift qualified the recipient to mount the steps of the portico, ring the bell, and be shown into the drawing-room by a liveried footman. Rabbits signified not only rabbit pie, but also a middling state in society. If refreshments were offered to side-door callers they were usually partaken of in the housekeeper's room or the butler's pantry; though there was a sub-division of this class: the village schoolmaster, postmaster, or a farmer who was a tenant, would be given a specially set tea in the library, shared only by the gentleman of the house. If Mr Purvis showed an intelligent interest in the squire's collection of coins, he would probably, as he wore a good suit and did not drop his h's, be so honoured.

Ordinary villagers, who received cans of soup as their appropriate share of the bounty, went as a matter of course to the back door and, after their business was concluded, were regaled, according to sex, with a mug of ale and what was known as "a bite" on the doorstep, or a cup of tea in the servants' hall. None who belonged to the two lower orders felt this grading at all derogatory. Many, if questioned, would have said they preferred to have it so, it made them feel "more comfortable, like". And the food and drink were good, even though the democratic spirit was defective.

But times and ideas were changing. By those Laura knew best at Heatherley their richer neighbours were regarded as customers, potential customers, or simply as people richer than themselves who happened to live near. Those poorer than themselves were people who might be glad to earn a shilling or two when they had a job of work to offer. The term "gentleman" was sometimes defined as one able and willing to pay twenty shillings in the pound, and as those who so defined it prided themselves on being able and willing to do likewise they had no feeling of inferiority. The poor still sometimes spoke of "the gentry", but having no longer anything to hope or fear from the class so described, they felt little interest in their doings. There was as yet no sign of class hostility; the classes had simply drawn apart, and were as natives of and dwellers in separate countries. The old order with its social prejudices, its assumption of superiority on the one hand and habitual self-abasement on the other, had fallen asunder, and with it had gone the old lavish hospitality and the warm human feeling which had bound man to man as members of one body. Other groupings and combinations of mankind were forming, but these still included only the few; each of the many fought for his own hand, hoping nothing and asking nothing but what he could grasp by his own effort. There was more widely diffused knowledge, though not noticeably more wisdom, and a new sense of independence was growing which was bound in the end to make for human dignity. The old social order had fallen and, though few then living realised it, the long and painful process of shaping the new was beginning. Of the fierce trials they and their children would have to endure before that process was completed, the men and women of that day had happily no foreboding.

'Garden of Girls'

The girl of that day—she then figured as *The Girl of Today* in heavy-type newspaper headings—was said to be mannerless, bold in her dress, speech, and deportment, without respect for her elders and devoid of feminine charm. Some professed to see in this sad falling-off a sign of the times. A dying century, they said, must naturally be a time of expiring virtues. Those whose manners and morals they condemned were degenerate children of a degenerate age. They spoke of modern youth as *fin de siècle,* pronounced in varying ways, but always with an inflection of disapproval.

Youth also applied to itself the term *fin de siècle,* as it did to most other things, for it was a favourite catchword of the day; but, applied to themselves by up-to-the-minute girls and young men, it signified self-congratulation rather than disparagement. New ideas and new ideals were in the air, blowing like a free, fresh wind—as they thought—through the old, stuffy atmosphere of convention, and what to their elders appeared as licence they gloried in as emancipation. In circles more advanced than that in which Laura moved the modern girl had already cast off some of her shackles. She had more freedom to think, speak, and act than her mother or grandmother had had at her age. Before the new century was far advanced, she believed, her freedom would be complete. The vote once secured for her sex, she and her fellow-women would be the equals of men in prestige and opportunity. Women's position in the home, too, would be a very different one when she was armed to fight for her own and her children's welfare.

But such ideas had not penetrated to country places. The girls Laura knew at Heatherley were *fin de siècle* only in the sense of having been born towards the end of the century. The New Woman, of course, they knew by repute, for she was a familiar figure to all the newspaper readers, usually depicted as hideous, in semi-masculine garb with hands extended to grab male privileges, while a balloon of print issuing from her mouth demanded "Votes for Women!" "Votes for Women?" fathers and brothers would say, "I'd give 'em votes if I had my way. I'd give 'em a good slapped bottom and make them stay at home, where they belong."

Mothers and elder sisters described the new women, not one of whom they had seen, as "a lot of great coarse, ugly creatures who can't get themselves husbands". "I'd rather see you in your coffin", parents told their daughters, "than wearing them bloomers and bawling for votes." Fortunately, no such choice was necessary. With such a warning before her as the current travesty of the "new woman" the average country girl determined to abstain altogether from ideas and concentrate upon being feminine.

Frilly muslin frocks, made long enough to sweep up the dust and to catch and tear on the bushes, flower-wreathed hats of floppy straw, long floating scarves, veils and streamers, were her ideal of womanly apparel. In her spare time she embroidered flowers with silks dyed in crude shades on chair-backs, hair-tidies, brush and nightdress cases, tea cosies, hot-water-can cosies and egg cosies, for what was known as her "bottom drawer", a collection of fancy articles it was then supposed to be the duty of every unmarried girl to amass, "against the time when she would have a home of her own". The girl who had acquired the largest and most varied collection of such articles was spoken of by her elders as a good, industrious girl who well deserved a good husband. What special advantage even the most closely packed bottom drawer was likely to be to a man was never stated. Laura was often called upon to inspect and admire the contents of such bottom drawers and she sometimes silently compared their proud owners to hen birds, hoarding straws before a mate appeared or the site of a nest was decided on.

The girls who were, as people said, "lucky" in getting husbands, had the satisfaction of using the contents of the bottom drawer to embellish their new homes. But not all were lucky. Laura had one friend who, having reached the age of twenty-six without having had what was known as "an offer", raffled the contents of her bottom drawer and bought a bicycle with the proceeds. The bicycle succeeded where the bottom drawer had failed. In six months she was married to the proprietor of a bicycle shop where she had stopped on one of her outings for some small repair. Whether or not she regretted parting prematurely with all her beautiful crewel and drawn-thread work nobody knew. Probably not, as she spent most of her married days helping her husband in his new and growing business and was reported to be making a small fortune teaching women and girls to ride their new bicycles.

All the world was awheel in those days. In London, society women and girls rode round and round in the parks in the morning, preferring the more novel form of exercise to riding on horseback in the Row. At weekends the suburbs poured their inhabitants into the country awheel. Sometimes, on a Sunday afternoon, Laura would go with some friend to the turning into the main road and watch the cyclists pass in a continual stream of twos, threes, and companies; the women riders in long skirts, made fast to their ankles with bands of elastic, and blouses with wide "bishop" sleeves, puffed out by the wind. Occasionally a woman in bloomers appeared, wearing a mannish felt hat with a long quill stuck bolt upright at the side, and a faint murmur of horror would go up from the beholders; but the wearers of bloomers were few, and the garment, which was seldom becoming to the middle-aged and often stout women who most affected it, was soon superseded by the divided skirt, an arrangement which had some kind of cleavage for riding, but fell to the feet in folds when the rider dismounted. The cyclists on that road came from the neighbouring towns. The Heatherley girls—except the engaged ones who, having a male escort, were privileged—did not, as they said, "go in for Sunday riding"; it was thought "common", and anything common was taboo.

So, on Sunday between church times, those who were as yet un-attached took gentle little walks in twos and threes and talked. More talking than walking was done. They would talk themselves to a standstill and find when the subject of their conversation was exhausted it was time to turn back. Those were the girls Laura knew best in the village—the daughters of shopkeepers, shop assistants and other business girls, whose parents kept apartment houses or farmed in a small way. There were also girls from other villages and from isolated homes on or about the heath, most of the girls living within easy walking distance and of about the same age and position in society being included in the set, or, as it was sometimes described, the "clique".

Most of them had had more educational advantages than Laura. A few had been to boarding schools; others to elementary schools which, being in the counties nearer London, were greatly in advance of those in remote rural districts, such as the one Laura had attended. They knew, at least by name, a variety of subjects which, as they said, they had "done" at school. But if such subjects had ever aroused any interest, it had faded, or turned to distaste. Occasionally, in the course of conversation, someone would supply a date, or the name of a city or river, or repeat parrotwise, a line or two from some popular poem, then exclaim: "But let's leave that dreary rot to the kids. Thank the gods and little fishes our school-days are over!"

Home and family life, the conscientious discharge of their duties and loyalty to their friends, were their strong points. There were born nurses among them and clever household managers, and almost without exception they knew how to make the best of their personal appearance and behave in a civilised manner.

They were essentially good girls, affectionate, helpful, and unselfish; they were good daughters and good sisters and were pre-pared to make good wives. They prided themselves upon their good-ness, as on their femininity. One of the poetical tags most frequently quoted was Kingsley's 'Be good, sweet maid, and let who will be clever', which was repeated with gusto on relevant occasions.

A good deal of sentimentality figured within the clique. Al-though friendly with all the circle, many of the girls had one special friend with whom they went everywhere and did everything. These pairs were recognised and seldom spoken of separately. It was

43

always "we must ask Maud and Fanny" or "Mary and Isobel". They walked with their arms round each other's waists, answered questions addressed to each other in conversation, and sometimes even dressed alike. Another piece of sentimentality common to the group was taken from Tennyson's song *Come into the Garden Maud.* 'A garden of girls' was their own private name for their association. "Another rosebud for our garden of girls" one of them would say quite seriously when some new acquaintance turned up. "Queen of our rosebud garden of girls!" another would exclaim of the wearer when a becoming new hat or frock appeared. It need scarcely be said that they took no interest whatever in abstract ideas, or indeed in anything which happened or existed outside their own radius. They aimed at being good, rather than intelligent, and in that perhaps they were typical of all but the more advanced girlhood of their day.

Those were the days when the pun still ranked as an acceptable form of humour. A pun, if it were a good pun, could still raise a laugh, or at least an indulgent smile, in circles far more intellectual than those open to Laura. But fashions in wit, like fashions in dress, can never survive extreme popularity, and at the turn of the century the pun had become too cheap to last much longer in favour. All who could articulate punned away merrily. Music hall stars, clergymen, fathers of families, servant girls, shopmen and butcher's boys. Even learned doctors and university dons were known to give way to this form of verbal frailty. From the lips of the girls Laura knew at that time puns dropped as profusely as gold, diamonds and pearls dripped from the lips of the girl in the fairy tale. One of Laura's lasting memories of Heatherley was that of making one of a cartload of girls returning from a picnic, packed three abreast on the front seat and three abreast on the back seat of an old-fashioned dog-cart; hats wreathed in pink roses, pink faces wreathed in smiles and bedewed with perspiration, and the pressure on each individual body similar to that of a large, warm, enveloping featherbed.

"We travelled at about this rate this morning," remarked one of the girls innocently, and another with a reputation for wit retorted: "What a tax on the wheels!" That was sufficient to set the whole cartload off wriggling and squealing with laughter, with the exception of one girl, slow at the uptake, into whose ear had to be hissed, "Rates and Taxes, you idiot; Rates and Taxes!" Her belated screech of laughter set the whole party off again and the cart had to be drawn to the side of the road and the old grey mare stopped while the girls dismounted and threw themselves down on the grass margin to cool off. One of the party, out of sheer high spirits, threw herself down with such abandon that she had to be told she was showing her legs. At that she sat up and clasped her hands tightly around her knees, for, as someone remarked, a man might have been coming along the road and seen her. Sobered by the mere idea, they all climbed back to their high seats and the driver chirruped her father's faithful old horse-of-all-work on its way through the dewy dusk, scented with heather and honeysuckle.

That was what now would be called a lowbrow party; one at the other extreme within the range was a book tea to which Laura was invited. The guests, she was told, were to wear or to bear something signifying a book title, and that was rather a worry to her because she knew some of the girls were planning something approaching fancy dress, which she could not possibly afford. Her first idea was to go as *The Woman in White*, but that would not do as her one white frock was a thin summer one and it was winter. Then she remembered she had a little brooch representing a windmill and that, pinned to her breast with a tassel of yellow floss silk, she thought might pass for *The Mill on the Floss*. Nobody guessed what it stood for, but then nobody guessed the meaning of half the symbols. A few were simple enough. One girl carried a small globe and that was plainly *The Wide Wide World*; another kissed and fondled a flaxen-haired doll, and those who had recently read the book exclaimed *"My Little Sweetheart"*. *Great Expectations* was represented by the facial expression of a guest who, on entering the room, pointed to the already laid tea-table and mimed pleasurable anticipation, then turned a little sulky when someone suggested *A Lunatic at Large*.

After an excellent tea in a house where cookery books were the favourite reading, the party played what they considered bookish games, such as cross questions and crooked answers. One, probably suggested by the article in the women's paper which had given the hostess the idea of the book tea, consisted of a series of questions to which each guest had to give a written answer.

> Do you prefer Dickens or Thackeray?
> Tennyson or Browning?

it began, then dropped suddenly in altitude to:

> White meat or brown?
> Apples or pears?
> Lilies or roses?

Dark or fair people?
Women or men?

which looked rather as if Muriel had substituted some of her own
ideas for those of the writer. However, the question game answered
its purpose of warming up the company and causing fun, and afterwards they went on to games not so bookish, such as I Spy and
Snap.

It was all very pleasant. The creature comforts were maybe
superior in quality to the intellectual entertainment. Such a warm,
softly padded room, such a glowing fire, such a dainty tea-table laid
with the family's best silver and china, and such superlative home-
made pork pies, cakes and scones, and muffins almost melting in the
best fresh butter!

Laura must have made special arrangements in order to go to
the book tea, unless it happened to be on a Bank Holiday, when she
and Alma had a free day alternately. But the girls who lived at home
and had no regular business hours went constantly to tea at each
other's houses, stampeding from house to house so frequently and
with such zest and jollity that they reminded Laura of the curates in
Shirley. At such times, to all appearances, not one of them had a
care in her heart or a thought in her head beyond that of having as
good a time as possible. "A heart like a balloon and a brain the size
of a gnat," snapped a cynical old friend of Laura's after she had told
him some little anecdote about the giver of one of the parties. But
although Laura applauded, she knew in her heart that human nature
cannot be simplified in that manner. As she came to know the girls
better she found that much of their frivolity and apparent brainless-
ness as a group was a pose, an unconscious pose, due to their
determination to appear wholly feminine. They had been told and
believed that serious thought was the prerogative of man; woman's
part in the scheme of creation was to be charming. Separately, each
of the girls had her own life to live, and for that both heart and brain
were necessary.

This was proved in after life by the very girl whose character
old Mr Foreshaw summed up in a sentence. She was certainly not
brilliant, though an unfortunate habit of giggling which she had at
that time made her appear less so than she actually was. When
called upon by circumstances, she proved capable of running her
dead father's little business and supporting her widowed mother in
comfort.

Then there was Patience, commonly called Patty, pink and plump and cheerful, who was always the one, when no man or youth was present, to collect the sticks and light the fire at a picnic. The other girls fought shy of this job for fear they should soil their light summer frocks, and before they had finished arguing as to who should do it Patty would have the fire lighted and, with her skirts kilted up, be down on her knees, blowing to encourage the feeble flame with her cheeks puffed out and her lips pursed like those of a cherub. Nobody ever accused Patty of butting in and spoiling their chance of a *tête-à-tête* with a young man who showed signs of being interested in themselves. Patty, they knew, would be more likely to say: "Now, you two, you just take a little stroll and leave me to see to these tea-things. But don't go that way. There's some of them having a game of rounders down there and they'll want you to play. You climb to the top of that hill and look at the view. And there's no call to hurry back. It'll take me some time to rinse out these cups and pack them, and when I've done that I shall take off my shoes and rest my poor feet, they do hurt me that cruel." And, when she had reduced chaos to order, Patty would rest in the shade and probably have a little nap, for she would have been up since four o'clock that morning to milk her father's three cows and earn her few hours of liberty by getting the housework done before breakfast. For Patty was the youngest and the only unmarried daughter of elderly parents and the work of the house and much of that of her father's small-holding was done by her. "A regular household drudge", was how some of her friends described her; but she did not think of herself as a drudge, she was too sweet-natured and willing.

And there was Edna, more fortunate in her worldly circumstances, but far less contented than Patty. Edna had a voice which her family and friends thought and often declared only needed training to rival that of Madame Patti. As no opportunity to have her voice trained had ever or was ever likely to come her way, Edna had to content herself with singing as leading soprano in the chapel choir and giving piano lessons at ninepence an hour to the village children. She often fretted over what she thought was a wicked waste of her gift; but perhaps she was more fortunate than she imagined, for her singing voice though capable of taking the high notes, was shrill and without a vestige of feeling. The test by a musical authority which she so much desired might have led to disillusionment while, as things were, her talent was highly esteemed in her own circle and was to herself a priceless possession on which to build daydreams.

Laura could sympathise with Edna, for she had, as she thought, a small gift of her own lying idle. From earliest childhood she had longed to write and, until the age of disillusionment set in, had been a great spoiler of paper. But since she had been at Heatherley and seen, and to some extent known, those she thought of as "real writers", she had felt ashamed of her own poor attempts and given up trying to write. Even her journal, begun on the day she first left home, had been discontinued. She had destroyed that with her other scraps of writing, saying to herself as they smouldered to tinder that that was the end of a foolish idea. But, after the folly had been renounced, there remained with her a sense of some duty neglected which almost amounted to a feeling of guilt, a feeling which persisted throughout her life whenever her pen was idle. She never spoke of this to anyone, but there the feeling was, like a pin pricking at her conscience. As her mother used to say, "we are as we are made".

While Edna's ambitions were respected by the other girls, Marion's made her the butt of the party. Marion was a large, serious, moonfaced girl who spent her working hours selling sweets and her spare time furthering a movement known as the Christian Endeavour. A new pastor at the chapel she attended had recently decided that, instead of listening to talks and addresses given by their elders or by some outside local celebrity, the members of the Christian Endeavour should themselves, in turn, prepare and deliver an address. Marion had apparently regarded the speakers at their Thursday evening meetings with awed respect. To speak in public was to her to have reached the very pinnacle of fame, a pinnacle to which she had never dreamed of aspiring. Now greatness was to be thrust upon her. On Thursday fortnight at 8 p.m., instead of merely carrying out her usual prized and jealously guarded office of placing on the table a glass of water at the speaker's elbow, she was herself to remain on the platform, deliver the address and sip the sacred water. It would be the first outstanding event in her life and she could think and talk of nothing else.

As the great day approached she went round with a little notebook and begged her friends to help her with suggestions. What subject should she choose? It need not be a religious subject, though, of course, it must be a serious one. Did Laura think 'Total Abstinence *versus* Moderation' would do? She had once heard an excellent address given under that title at the Band of Hope and thought she could remember most of it. Laura advised something that would be new to her listeners and casually suggested 'The Sweets of Life', thinking she might draw upon her experiences in her sweet shop to provide a little light relief before drawing the moral that the best things in life cost nothing. Marion adopted the idea with enthusiasm. But deciding on a subject, she soon found, was but a beginning; she had still to compose her address. And that was what she could not do. She would write a few sentences, never, even in her large sprawling handwriting, filling more than one sheet of notepaper; hand round what she had written to be read, then alter or cross out according to the advice she received. The fortnight became a week and the week a few days and she had still written so little that it could have been read aloud in one minute. She was a great fat girl whom no amount of worry could have made thin, but her lips began to droop at the corners and her large, round face looked quite woebegone. Laura grew tired of seeing her come into the post office and of having that notebook thrust under her nose. Alma criticised Marion's behaviour as freely as Laura did, but hers was constructive criticism. She it was who put an end to Marion's worry and her friends' boredom by offering to go one evening to Marion's home and help her to write the address.

That done, Marion bloomed again. Her new frock came home in good time from the dressmaker; she resumed her air of importance, practised her gestures, including the sipping of water from an imaginary glass, before her mirror, and finally astonished her friends by ordering a cab to take her from her home to the lecture hall. "But why a cab, Marion?" said everyone, "it's such a short walk, and you never have a cab to take you to the meetings, or even to the Annual Social." But Marion was quite decided on that subject. She had seen and heard speakers from outside the village arrive in a cab and evidently in her opinion the scrunching of cab wheels on the gravel and the gleam of cab lamps through the open door of the hall where the audience was already assembled were necessary to extract the full flavour of the honour and glory of the occasion. And who could begrudge her that last touch of importance on her night of nights? Unless in the same way, she was not likely ever to be in the limelight again, for she was not a marrying kind of girl. "Too big and clumsy and silly-simple", the other girls decided when discussing her prospects. The last time Laura saw Marion she was closing, with a twirl, a bag of sweets to refresh Laura on a train

49

journey, and she may still be twirling sweet-bags, or she may by this time be a doting grandmother, for when it comes to chances of matrimony you never can tell.

Edna and Marion were exceptions and as such stand out in the memory. The main preoccupation of most of the girls was getting themselves a husband and planning matches for their friends. For, as yet, no ordinary girl was disposed to dispute the general ruling that the success or failure of a woman's life depended on marriage. If a good marriage in a worldly sense, so much the better, but any ordinary marriage was regarded as success in life, and even a poor one as better than spinsterhood. In spite of shining examples of single life in every station, the unmarried woman, or old maid, was looked down upon with a mixture of pity and contempt. The headmistress of a school, the hospital matron, or the proprietress or manageress of a successful business, if unmarried, was classed among those who had failed in the main object of life; while those without any such abilities would, so long as they wore a wedding ring, speak patronisingly of them.

Laura, like other girls of her time, regarded as a matter of course her marriage some day in the future. From her earliest childhood she had heard people say that, for a woman, a married life was the only natural life. "Better a bad husband than no husband at all" was a proverb among the countrywomen around her home. While she was still in her teens, when quoting it for her benefits they would sometimes add reassuringly: "But you needn't be afraid. You'll get married all right. You're one of the quiet sort men like for a wife", and when in reply Laura would shake her head and declare that she did not mean to marry, "ever", they would laugh and say, "All right, my girl. I've heard that tale before. You wait until Mr Right comes along. When he says 'snip' you'll say 'snap' fast enough, I'll warrant." When she had turned twenty and still had the appearance of no Mr Right to report, their remarks were less kindly. "What, twenty, and no sweetheart yet!" exclaimed one old friend. "You'd better look out for one or you'll be left on the shelf", and when at the age of twenty-four Laura was at last about to be married the same old neighbour said feelingly: "Well, I am glad! I really am! What a blessing you've been lucky at last! I was really afraid you were going to be one of the leftovers!"

Much the same ideas ruled at Heatherley, though less pointedly expressed, and the girls who had their homes there must sometimes have been, as Laura was, irritated by other people's interest in their affairs. But most of them appeared to take kindly to the notion of marriage as an aim in life, and in the end most of them did marry. Whether more or less wisely for knowing that marriage was expected of them cannot be said.

Those who failed, or failed for some time, to fulfil that expectation, sometimes suffered. There was the case of Izzy. A few years before Laura knew her she had been by general consent the established beauty of the neighbourhood. Her dark, wavy hair, grey-blue eyes, and slim, straight figure still held an air of distinction against the general pink and white plumpness of other girls. But Izzy by that time was twenty-seven and well on the way to old maidenhood. Unless she married Eric. A much discussed question among the girls in her absence was, will Izzy marry, or will her unsatisfactory engagement drag on for years, only to peter out in the end? There were some who said she was already married, that she wore her wedding ring on a ribbon round her neck beneath her clothes and that she and Eric were only waiting for his father to die before proclaiming themselves man and wife before the world. One girl actually said she had seen the wedding ring, or at least a bit of the ribbon upon which it was suspended, peeping out from the neck of her blouse. But Izzy was not married. She would probably have been a happier girl if she had been, even secretly.

Izzy and her widowed mother lived by letting apartments in the neighbouring settlement. In the summer months they took in holiday visitors; one of their front parlours accommodated the village branch of a Bank, and they had, as a permanent boarder, a middle-aged business manager. They were fairly prosperous and Izzy, as a child and a young girl, had been much indulged by her mother, who adored her. While she was still in her teens, her mother had set her heart on "my little Izzy", or "my one ewe lamb" as she called her, making a good match. Her favourite idea was that some rich and distinguished summer visitor to their house would fall in love with and marry her. Such things had been known to happen. Not being of a very reserved or a very discreet nature, she had confided her hopes to neighbouring gossips who had soon made them public.

But by the time Laura knew Izzy her mother's hopes of a grand match for her had faded. For Izzy had become what the other girls described as "mixed up" with a young man whose father had livery stables in the district. In those days, before the advent of the motor car, a livery stable was a profitable and important business. The proprietor would own horses and vehicles, saddle-horses for hacking, horses and carriages for general hire, and often a horse-bus running between the station and town. He would provide, even if he did not actually own, a pair of greys for a wedding couple, or a pair of blacks with flowing manes and tails to draw a hearse. He would employ stablemen and drivers, wear smart, horsey clothes, and often be inclined to look down on the ordinary tradesman. Such a man was Eric's father. Eric himself was a good-looking fellow who, in his smart Bedford cords and well-polished leggings, sat his horse with the air of a gentleman of leisure. Almost daily he rode up to one of the heaths near Heatherley and there Izzy would meet him, when he would dismount, take his horse's reins over his arm and stroll by her side, the two in deep converse. When they first walked so they had no doubt talked of and schemed for their marriage. In hopeful moods they may still have done so, for hope is a perennial plant which can thrive on little nutriment, but in more sober moments they must both of them have realised the hopelessness of their position. For Eric had neither money nor prospects, beyond the far distant prospect of inheriting the family business, which was not one to set up house upon when his father was still in the prime of life and as strong looking and almost as young looking as his son.

Mr Tolman was one of the, even then, almost obsolete type of business men who expected their sons, and of course their daughters, to stay at home and work in the family business without wages. It was said among the girls that Eric had once asked his father to pay him some stated sum, if but a pound a week, and that his answer had been: "What the devil do you want with wages? You're master here, as much as I am myself; why want to turn yourself into a stableman! You have the run of your teeth in the house and a first-class suit from my own tailor whenever you need it, and a pound or two here and there to put in your pocket. Where's the need of anything more! What would you do with it if you got it? Go running up to town on a Saturday night, or get mixed up with some hussy round here! Keep all the money we can get in the business is my motto, as it was my father's and grandfather's before me. Left like that, money breeds money, and it'll all be yours somewhen."

So Eric had no income at all that he could depend upon. Five pounds from his father when he had brought off a good deal in horseflesh, a pound or two saved by his mother from the house-keeping money and handed to him secretly, and a guinea now and again from a riding pupil, kept him well supplied for his personal expenses. He had money in his pocket to back a horse or to stand a drink for a friend; he gave Izzy some handsome presents and was never wanting in such delicate little attentions as bringing her flowers, or sweets, or bottles of scent. But he could not marry.

He was himself of a happy-go-lucky nature, and with good looks, a comfortable home, and money in his pocket he would have been very well satisfied with his lot in life had it not been for his relations with Izzy. He loved her truly and wanted to marry her, but he did not see the necessity for an immediate marriage. "You've got a good home and so have I," he told her, "so where's the hurry? It'll all come right in the end you'll find. You know I'll be true to you, don't you, Izzy?" In the meantime, Izzy's slight figure became angular, her shoulders higher, and her features sharper. Some of the girls began to speak of her as a killjoy at their merrymakings, but she still joined them occasionally and regained some of her old spirits in their company.

In these more rational days a girl in Izzy's position would long before either have made a clean break in the relationship or have cheerfully accepted it as a pleasant friendship, binding on neither. But Izzy was of a loving and constant nature; with her it was Eric or nobody, and it is not at all likely that the thought of mere friendship between them ever occurred to her. At that time and in that class of society friendship between a man and a woman was rare. The very idea was scoffed at by many as something unnatural. A man, it was said, wanted but one thing of a woman and that should be sought by way of wedlock. As to a girl who encouraged such a friendship, she was as bad as the man, or she was a fool, letting her youth and her chances slip by. A hard ruling for the few who happened to have interests outside sex, but one which had to be abided by, for if flouted, there were unpleasant results in the form of gossip and the alienation of friends.

The young of either sex, who naturally inclined towards each other, often by-passed this ban on friendship by entering into hasty and ill-considered engagements and the breaking off of such an engagement when found distasteful by either party was made painful by public opinion. If the man broke it off, and it was usually the man who did so, he was said to be a villain who had jilted the poor girl; if the girl, she was either a heartless flirt or a fool who would live to regret her wicked, unwomanly action. A girl whose erstwhile lover had taken the initiative was in the most unenviable position, for she was the object of a contemptuous kind of pity which was most hurtful to her pride.

In those days breach-of-promise cases were numerous and the newspapers made a special feature of them, reported in detail and embellished with sketches of the principal parties. The hearing of an involved case would often last for days and provide for those following the proceedings in their newspapers both entertainment and a subject for conversation. Many took sides, the men usually sympathising with the man in the case and the women with the woman. In this way the idea of transmuting injured feelings into hard cash, and at the same time avenging one's wrongs by bringing unwelcome publicity upon the offender, became a familiar one. No-one Laura knew personally was ever involved in such an action, but she often heard of the threat of bringing one being held, like a rod taken out of pickle, over the head of a defaulting lover. One un-forgettable scene she witnessed was that of seeing a quiet, modest, amiable girl who had been what was then known as jilted, in the midst of weeping into her handkerchief and bewailing her woes, suddenly spring to her feet, cast her sopping handkerchief aside, crying belligerently, "I'll make him suffer for this, you mark my words I will. I'll breach him! I'll breach him!" The effect was that of a little bleating shorn lamb suddenly ramping and rearing in incongruous rage. But of course Millicent did not carry out her threat. Instead, she mildly and patiently lived down the gossip she had dreaded, and in time found another and let us hope a more constant lover. This might have been expected by anyone who knew her, and the wonder is how the other idea arose in her quiet, gentle mind and was given such fierce expression.

Except for such complications in a few cases, the lives of the Heatherley girls ran smoothly from protected childhood to carefree youth and on to protected marriage, and that, as a general rule, was all they asked of life. But later, life must have made great demands upon many of them, for the girls of that day became the mothers of the young soldiers in the First World War. How they met the trials which then faced them Laura did not know, for she had long before lost touch with them, but there need be no doubt that their genuine goodness of heart enabled them to bear all that was laid upon them, and that their old gaiety of spirit, by that time sobered to a steady cheerfulness, supported others as well as themselves in the day of trouble and mourning. There is a lot to be said for, as well as a little against, the old-fashioned womanly woman.

Mr Foreshaw

The friends thought most suitable for Laura by her elders were those of her own age, sex, and social condition, and at Heatherley she had several such friends whose company she enjoyed and whose good qualities she appreciated. But like herself, these had had little experience of life, their views and interests were limited, and she often longed to meet someone with a wider mental horizon. Gradually, while still at Heatherley, she did find a few other friends, less suitable for her according to the conventional ruling, but who, she herself felt, gave a new, keen relish to life. The earliest and most memorable of these was Mr Foreshaw.[21]

Laura had often noticed a distinguished-looking old gentleman with snow-white hair and a small, neatly-trimmed white beard at the post office counter. He was tall and, except for a slight droop of his shoulders, fairly erect; but when seen closely, his great age was apparent in his dark, dried, deeply wrinkled face and forehead, and his eyes which, beneath shaggy brows, were ringed with white round the iris. In winter he wore a long, thick black overcoat and a seal-skin cap with ear-pieces tied down under his chin. In hot summer weather he would sometimes appear in a white drill suit of tropical cut.

"Who is the old gentleman in the white suit?" Laura one day asked Alma, who, having her home there, knew most people who lived in the village, and she was told that her old gentleman's name was Mr Foreshaw, and that a year or two before he had had a bungalow built for himself at the end of a little lane off the main road, where he had since lived alone. That was all Alma knew about him, and she was sure to know all that was generally known in the village, so who Mr Foreshaw was, where he had lived and what he had done before coming to Heatherley, and why in extreme old age he had elected to live alone, for some time remained to Laura a mystery. But she, loving a mystery, and being exceptionally fond of aged people, still felt a great interest in her old man, as Alma called him, and would show him any little attention she could when he came to the post office. Disregarding rules and regulations, she would take the letters from his awkward, arthritic old hands and stick on the stamps for him, and soon, if she were on duty, he would as a matter of course pass over to her his unstamped letters. But, beyond thanking her, he said little, and that little was said so gruffly and abruptly that she thought that for some unknown cause he did not like her. One day Alma, who by that time had collected a little more information about him, told Laura that Mr Foreshaw was known to be a woman-hater. He would not have a woman in his house even to clean it and cook his meals, but employed for those purposes an elderly ex-serviceman.

Then one evening after the office door had been locked and while Laura was putting on her hat to go home a telegram came off, addressed to 'Foreshaw, The Bungalow'. From the contents of the

---

[21] See Notes at end of book for a possible identity of Mr Foreshaw

telegram it appeared that someone named Roberts was arriving by a late train that night. The telegraph messengers had gone home and could not be recalled as it was past their working hours. Laura should not have taken off the telegram after eight o'clock, but her response to the musical tinkle of Heatherley's code letters had become automatic. Now she had the telegram on her hands. If it had been for any other address she would not have thought twice before setting out herself to deliver it, as she had often before delivered late-coming messages which appeared to be urgent; but in view of Mr Foreshaw's reputation as a woman-hater, she hesitated. He might not appreciate even so small a voluntary service by one of her sex.

But there lay the telegram in its orange-coloured envelope; Mr Foreshaw's visitor was about to step into the railway carriage at Waterloo station; and at the bungalow, Mr Foreshaw was probably thinking of going to bed. The old people she had known hitherto had all gone to bed very early. To save light and fire, they said, and because there was nothing else to do, and they would have been alarmed if knocked up by a visitor at midnight. She slipped the telegram into the pocket of her coat and stepped out into the warm dusk of the August evening.

"At the very end of the lane, standing back in a garden, you'll find it", the man had said of whom she asked the way, and when she came to the gate, she knew she had found it, because in a lighted room, with the curtains undrawn and the window wide open, she could see Mr Foreshaw himself in a grey dressing-gown and black velvet smoking-cap, sitting at a table spread with papers. In response to her timid knock he came to the door. "What's this?" he said. "What? A telegram? Ah, now I see who it is. Come in. Come in. I can't read it here in the darkness." Laura stepped before him into the lighted room and he, after courteously drawing forward a chair for her, sank back into his former seat before the maps, for she saw now that the sheets spread out upon the table were maps, upon which, as she was shown afterwards, he had marked in red ink the course of his many journeys.

As he read the telegram Mr Foreshaw's bushy white eyebrows rose considerably. "Roberts? Roberts?" he ejaculated. "Ah, now I recollect the fellow. Saw him last in the Zambesi valley in '84. Good of him to look me up. Don't get many visitors these days. Not that I've got any burning desire for 'em, too used to my own company. Very good of you to bring the wire. You must have a drink now you're here."

The offer of a drink rather alarmed Laura, for she barely knew the name of any drink other than beer, which she did not like; but interest, or curiosity, made her glad of any excuse to stay a little longer and she said that she would like a little water, or milk, if he had it to spare. At that he laughed gruffly and said that he had not suspected her of being a milk and watery miss, and milk he had not, never touched the stuff, and as to giving her water, he'd leave that sort of hospitality to good Christian people. He's an old pagan, thought Laura, a regular old pagan, and repeated the word mentally with some pride, for she had but recently discovered its modern usage. "But I've got something here I think you will like", he continued, and he brought a bottle out of a cupboard and mixed her a tumblerful of some sweet syrup and water, which she sipped appreciatively.

Mr Foreshaw sat at the table, propping his head upon one hand, his eyes from beneath their bushy eyebrows regarding her, as she thought critically, though kindly. The fresh night air from without billowed the window-curtains and stirred the papers upon the table, and every pause in the conversation was filled with the loud tick-tocking of the clock in the hall. Laura had never before seen a room at all like Mr Foreshaw's. The light green walls had not a single picture, only framed maps, and here and there long hangings like narrow curtains upon which stiff, angular figures of men and beasts were silhouetted in black on a white ground. On the mantelpiece stood a few pieces of queer foreign-looking pottery and an ostrich's egg upon which someone had drawn a pen-and-ink sketch of an ostrich with a man's face. A tall bookcase stood on one side of the fireplace, the recess on the other side had a stand on which were arranged spears, blowpipes and other weapons, and all about the room stood glass-topped showcases containing specimens of some kind. But that night Laura had time for no more than a general impression of her surroundings, for she feared she was intruding upon Mr Foreshaw's privacy, and after draining her glass she rose and said she was sure he had much to attend to before his visitor arrived. At that he laughed and said, "Airing a bed for Roberts and getting out the best linen and china you mean, eh? No, no, that's not how we old bachelors manage things. Roberts is an old campaigner like myself and as long as the tantalus and tumblers are on the table he will be satisfied."

A few days later Mr Foreshaw, handing over his letters to be stamped, rumbled: "When are you coming to see me again? If you've got nothing better to do come on Sunday and pour out my tea. If anybody asks you where you are going tell 'em to visit your aged grandfather." Fortunately, Laura had no one to whom it was necessary to account for her movements and she went to see Mr Foreshaw many times. At the time of his first invitation Alma was present and heard what he said and Laura's reply. After he had gone she was a little discouraging. "You and your old man!" she said, "I can't understand you, really. If you feel like going out to tea anywhere why not come to us, up home, and go for a walk with Arthur and me afterwards." But that programme, though kindly offered, did not appeal to Laura, who thought making a third in a lovers' walk a tame prospect compared to a visit to the bungalow. After that, Alma was always a little cold and reserved when any mention was made of Mr Foreshaw, but she was not a gossiping girl and unlikely to have discussed Laura's eccentricity in friendship with others. If anyone else at any time saw her slip up the little green lane and through the white gate at the end of it they probably thought that Mr Foreshaw's great age exempted her from the rule of the day that no really nice girl should ever go alone to the house of a man. But it was far more likely that no-one other than Alma knew of her visits to the bungalow.

On her second visit to him Mr Foreshaw showed Laura his trophies, including his glass cases of tropical butterflies with wings of the most glorious colours, as bright and fresh as if newly painted, but with wings and bodies so stiff and motionless and so imprisoned under the glass that the sight made her feel sad. "Pretty things," he said, "you like them, eh?" and she, gazing down on them, each one with a pin through its middle and a little label beneath with its name and its species, could think of no better answer than, "I should like to see them alive." There were cases of mineral specimens and of arrow heads, stuffed crocodile skins, horns and hoofs, and rugs made of the skins of beasts he had shot in his big-game hunting days. For Mr Foreshaw had for thirty years been a professional big-game hunter in British and Portuguese East Africa. That, he told Laura when he knew her better, was why he had never married. "Didn't want to leave some poor woman crying her eyes out every time I disappeared into the blue", he said; "bad for a man, too, cripples his nerve. 'He rides swiftest who rides alone', as that new young feller, Kipling, puts it."

Almost every article in his large collection had a story. There was a tusk of the elephant he had shot that time when the platform of boughs and leafy twigs upon which he was standing collapsed; when he fell to the ground, right in the path of the wounded charging animal, it had seemed as if the next moment he would be trampled to death. His "boys", as he called his native carriers, scattered in all directions, "like streaks of greased lightning", he said. But the poor beast, blinded with its own blood, staggered aside as it passed him and, a few yards farther on, collapsed. "A damned near thing that time," was his comment when telling the story. He had had number-less such narrow escapes, from wild animals met suddenly in un-expected places, from snake bite, and from hostile native tribes. Once he had been chased by a pack of wild dogs and, having taken refuge in the boughs of a tree, had to remain there for over three hours with the creatures leaping and snapping just short of his feet. Twice he was deserted by his carriers, and once during a great drought he and his party almost perished of thirst.

He told Laura stories of many such tight corners. When, in the course of their conversation, he said, "Once, when I was in the Zambesi valley," or "in Portuguese East", or "prospecting for minerals in the Transvaal", Laura knew there was a story coming. Once she ventured to ask him if, after such an adventurous life, he did not find Heatherley dull, and he replied with his characteristic grunt, which by one more experienced than Laura might have been recognised as an exclamation of suppressed suffering, "Dull? Yes, damned dull. I feel old and cold and as dull as ditchwater and I shan't be sorry to go. Go where? Well, wherever old hunters do go when they die. Pity they can't be like the old elephants who, when they feel their time coming, go alone into the bush, or a swamp, and take what's coming to 'em without a lot of bother and fuss. Did I ever tell you I once found an elephants' cemetery? That was in a swamp. Tons of ivory! I had my boys digging for a fortnight, then made a special journey to Beira to ship off the tusks and to blue most of the proceeds. That was the time I saw with my own eyes the Hindoo kill, pluck and roast a chicken and burn the feathers, then bring it back to life again. Heard the thing's death squawk, saw its blood run when he cut its throat, smelt the roasting flesh and the feathers burning, take my oath I did! Then saw the live fowl running and cackling afterwards. No conjuring about it. Ground as bare as the palm of my hand for yards around and the fellow practically naked. Just him and the bird and a little stick fire. How do I think it was done? Now you're asking something! Some say it's mesmerism. Fowl never killed, and of course never roasted; just a few feathers burnt, and the rest takes place in the imagination of the spectators, suggested by the performer of course. In my opinion it's just pure magic. Yes, I believe in magic, and so would you if you had seen what I've seen. Ever hear of the Indian rope trick? Never had the luck to see that myself, but I've known men willing to swear on the Bible they'd seen it, and not particularly hard-drinking men either."

When Laura came to know Mr Foreshaw better she rallied him on his reputation as a woman-hater. He laughed, grunted, and said: "Not a hater of women between the ages of fifteen and fifty, excepting the weasels and quacks, as we used to call 'em, meaning the dried-up, vinegarish sort and the fat white waddlers. Those I never cared for. Girl children I must admit I'm not particularly fond of, and as to old women of either sex, I" (grinding his teeth) "absolutely abominate 'em."

For nearly a year Laura went at least once a week to see Mr Foreshaw. On many Sunday afternoons she sat opposite him at the table at which she had first seen him sitting over his maps, and ate guava jelly, dried ginger, or some other dainty he had brought out from his store-cupboard, with cream in her tea, while he drank black coffee and nibbled a dry biscuit.

From the first Laura liked Mr Foreshaw. She liked him for his originality, his raciness, his immense store of experience and his biting wit. As she came to know him better and to realise what a trial it must be to him to live such a quiet, inactive life, after his years of stirring adventure, old and alone and often in pain, her liking deepened to affection. And she thought Mr Foreshaw liked her. The way he treated her was, she knew, partly due to his courteous, old-fashioned manners; but to her, unused as she was to such consideration, it was delightful to have someone take care that she had a comfortable seat, did not sit in a draught, to have her permission to smoke asked at each pipe-lighting, and to have her slightest need elaborately supplied at table. If she called in the evening, when she left he would apologize for not being able to enjoy the great pleasure of seeing her home safely, and even in cold weather he would stand in the doorway until the gate had closed behind her, then raise his hand in a last salute.

On the day of her first visit to tea he had shown her a room, saying: "Here is a little bower for you if you want to curl your hair or anything. It is a long time since I entertained a lady, so if I have forgotten anything you must put my forgetfulness down to my old bachelor ways; but you will find a looking-glass there, and I've put you out a bottle of eau de cologne ...."

"And a paper of pins!" exclaimed Laura, "and it's all just lovely! I feel like Mrs Micawber when she went to supper with David." Which was a happy remark of hers, for he was a great lover of Dickens and, he then told her, had always carried his books with him on his expeditions. He showed her the book he had been reading that afternoon before she arrived. It was a copy of *Great Expectations,* and the small round holes like shot-holes which pierced the back cover and tunnelled through the pages had been bored by white ants.

The fiction of Dickens, Thackeray, and a few other Victorians was still his favourite reading, though he also read a good deal of travel and biography and every new book which appeared about Africa. With the one exception of Kipling, whose short stories he greatly admired, he did not care for the modern novelists. "These new men," as he called them, "setting up their Aunt Sallies and shyin' at 'em, and damned clumsy about it, with their little knotty points they call problems, which the older writers would have taken in their stride!"

Laura came to know Mr Foreshaw well and her contact with him, though but of short duration, made a lasting impression on her mind. Yet, looking back in after years, she was surprised that she had learned so little about his life. He would talk freely about his thirty years of big-game hunting in Africa, but of his life before and after that period he said not a word. Where he had been born and spent his childhood, who were his parents, and whether or not he had relatives still living at the time she knew him, she was not told. She did not know if he had loved, or experienced sorrow, beyond the affection he had felt for the lion and cheetah cubs he had reared and kept as pets, and the sorrow he had felt when he lost them, either by death, or by having to ship them off to some zoo in Europe when they became too big and too "playful" to suit his carriers. All she knew of his private life was that he had, or had had, a sister, and she knew that only because she had read on the fly-leaf of one of his books, *Charles Foreshaw, from his loving sister Clara. Christmas 1880.*

If still living, his sister never came to see him, nor did he ever mention her. Except the doctor, who besides his professional visits sometimes came in the evening to play chess with him, the only visitor he had besides herself while Laura knew him was the Roberts of the telegram, who had stayed two nights and immediately afterwards returned to South Africa where he had many years before his visit married the widowed owner of a hotel in Rhodesia.

Nor did Mr Foreshaw know much about Laura. She had told him a little about her parents and home and he had seemed interested, and he always enjoyed hearing about any amusing little incident which occurred in her present daily life. But Laura was a listener rather than a talker, and there were whole tracts in her life and nature that he could not have suspected. They had a similar sense of humour and both thought some things funny which others thought sad, and sad that others thought funny, and that perhaps was the closest bond between them. Only once did she see him moved. Then they had been talking of ghosts and he had been condemning spiritualists and spiritualism, while Laura wavered a little and said that perhaps, after all, there might be something in it. She had heard some strange stories in childhood of people seeing what appeared to be spirits, people she had known and whose word she could believe.

"Ah, there you are," he said, "superstition, thy name is woman! I'll bet you'd be afraid to live in this bungalow after I had died in it. Afraid I'd haunt you, eh?" and Laura, a little offended at being thought superstitious, protested that she felt sure she would never fear the ghost of anyone she had known and been fond of. If it were possible, which she doubted, as he did, she thought that she would want to see them.

"But you never will, never! That's the devilishness of death. I knew a man who, towards the end of a trip, sent one of his boys in advance down to the coast to collect his mail. When the letters came, there was one among them—well, someone he knew had died—and I tell you that man prayed all that night, prayed on his knees, mind you, that the spirit of his friend might appear to him, just once. He asked no more than to see her face once again. And what happened? Nothing. Absolutely nothing. Outside his tent in the darkness the palm leaves rattled in the slight breeze that always comes in those parts just before dawn. That, and the loud snoring of his boys huddled round the embers of the camp fire, were the only sounds that he heard. Not a whisper from her, nor a sign to tell that, though unseen, she was near him; only emptiness, emptiness everywhere!"

Mr Foreshaw sank back, his swollen old hands grasping the arms of his chair. Laura said nothing. What could she say? She could only look her sympathy. When he spoke again it was in his ordinary tone about some small everyday matter. But that evening, before she left him, he said "I should like you to live here when I have gone and take care of my things. Shan't be allowed to take 'em with me, and don't like the idea of them being scattered and knocked about by strangers."

But that was just what did happen to Mr Foreshaw's trophies. One morning the news ran round the village that the old gentleman up at the bungalow had died in his sleep. The ex-service man who cleaned and cooked for him had found him, looking as peaceful as a child asleep, he had told people, and the doctor had said that it was no more than he had expected, as that rheumatic complaint affected the heart.

The doctor and a lawyer from town were the only mourners at his funeral and their two wreaths were the only flowers placed upon his coffin. To those wired, waxen florist's flowers, when they lay on his grave, another friend added a bunch of red roses, chosen because she knew he had loved deep, rich colour in flowers, as he had loved everything strong, warm and positive in life.

After long search, as it appeared, a great-nephew of Mr Foreshaw was discovered in Canada, and as legal heir to the property he gave instructions that the bungalow and its contents should be sold by auction. On the evening of the day of the sale Laura, at the post-office window, watched women passing by carrying curtains, china, lamps and fire-irons, and men trundling the heavier furniture on wheelbarrows. A boy marched past with a pair of branching antlers held to his own forehead, and two girls swung carelessly between them a clothes-basket containing cups and saucers.

It was some consolation to Laura to learn that his collection of butterflies and some of his native weapons and pottery had been bought by the curator of a museum. Those, at least, would not be "knocked about", though the story attached to almost every article having now gone to the grave with their former owner, they would become mere objects of interest.

Laura made a timid bid for one of her old friend's books. A woman had come into the post office and placed on the counter while she made her purchases a bundle of books, tied ruinously tightly with string and marked "Lot 39", which she said she had bought for a shilling, though what she was going to do with them when she got home she did not know, she had only bought them because they were going so cheaply. Laura touched a copy of *Vanity Fair* with her forefinger. It had been a favourite book with Mr Foreshaw, who had always maintained that Becky Sharp would have been a better woman if she had been born to her ten thousand a year. As it was, he liked her for her mettle.

"Would you care to sell me this one for a shilling?" asked Laura, and the woman had replied tartly, "No. If it's worth a shilling to you it's worth a shilling to me. I'll keep it to prop open my pantry window."

Although his fears had proved true as to the fate of his possessions, Mr Foreshaw's own ending had been such as he would have wished. Like the old elephant which had staggered away beneath its weight of years to die in the swamp, he also had died alone, without "fuss and bother". Laura had lost a kind friend, one whose like she felt she would scarcely meet again, and she was both saddened and sobered. It was the first time in her life that she felt a sense of personal loss. People she had known had died and she had felt sorry, but none of them had been near to her; she had never before faced the great dark, silent abyss which lies between the dead and the living. For weeks after Mr Foreshaw's death, when anything interesting or amusing occurred or was said, she would think, "I must tell that to Mr Foreshaw", then realise sadly that she would never again tell him anything, or hear his shrewd, spicy comments.

The Wind on the Heath

Her work at the post office, making new friends and reading new library books in quick succession, did not fill the whole of Laura's life at this time. She had another interest which, though she was able to devote less time to it, lay nearer her heart's core.

Her love of nature was an inborn love and she was quick to recognise natural beauty even in those places where such beauty was not spectacular. In her own county, where the landscape as a whole was plain and homely, there were many sweet scenes which were dear to her. Buttercup meadows set round with dark elms, deep double hedgerows white with may, festooned with wild rose or honeysuckle, or berried with hips and haws and hung with big silvery puffs of old-man's-beard, according to season. And there were little brooks, banked with willow herb and meadowsweet, which meandered through fields where in spring skylarks soared and sang above the young green wheat or patches of bright yellow mustard; and later in the year when the small birds were silent and coveys of young partridge chicks scurried *peep-peeping* to cover before an approaching footstep on the field paths, those same fields would be golden with ripe grain and there would be poppies in the corn.

And since she had left home, although she had not actually seen the sea, she had seen an Essex saltmarsh bluish-mauve with sea lavender, and a tidal river with red fisher sails upon it and gulls wheeling overhead and seaweed clinging to the stones of its quays. All those things she had loved and would always love. If she had been condemned to live in a great city for the rest of her life they would still have been hers, for nothing could rob her of such memories.

Her love of her own county was that of a child for its parent, a love which takes all for granted instinctive rather than inspiring, but lifelong. Her love of the Heatherley countryside was of a different nature. It had come to her suddenly in that moment of revelation when, on the day of her arrival she had unexpectedly come out on the heath and seen the heather in bloom. She had felt then a quick, conscious sense of being one with her surroundings, and as she came to know the hills and heaths in all moods and seasons, the feeling became more definite. It was more a falling in love on her part than of merely loving.

After she had become established at Heatherley her greatest pleasure in life was in her few free daylight hours to roam on the heather-clad hills or to linger in one of the valley woods where trickling watercourses fed the lush greenery of ferns and bracken and mosses and the very light which filtered down through the low, matted overgrowth was tinged with green. She liked best to walk in those places alone, for although she soon made a few friends, a walk in their company, she found, meant a brisk swinging progress from point to point to the accompaniment of much talk and laughter. Such walks could be taken on dark evenings after the office was closed and they were then often taken by Laura with great enjoyment. But she loved best her solitary walks, when she could stand and gaze at some favourite viewpoint, watch the heath birds and insects and quick-darting lizards, gather the heath flowers into little stiff honey-scented bouquets, run the warm, clean heath sands through her fingers and bare her head to the soft, misty rain.

Sunday morning, after the office had closed, was the best time, and in winter the only time for these solitary walks. With good luck in the matter of work, she would have her hat and coat already on when the telegraph instrument ticked out its daily message from Greenwich: *"T-i-m-e—T-i-m-e—T-i-m-e"*, then, after a few seconds' pause, "T-E-N!" A moment later she would have locked the door behind her and be halfway down the village street on her way to the hills or woods. During the Boer War, with wireless broadcasts far in the future and only very early editions, printed the day before, of the Sunday newspapers reaching many places, the Government authorities thought it necessary to institute Sunday morning bulletins giving the latest war news. These were tele-graphed to every post office to be written out and displayed in the post-office windows. The bulletin was supposed to arrive before ten o'clock, when the offices closed. Occasionally it did arrive before ten, but far more often, at Heatherley, it came a quarter, a half, or sometimes a whole hour after that time. Laura, who had no objection on other days to staying beyond her hours to complete this or that, found this involuntary Sunday overtime exasperating, for it shortened her walk.

When, sooner or later, she was at liberty, it took her but a few minutes to reach open country. Looking neither to right nor left lest she should see some acquaintance who would volunteer to come with her, she would rush like a bandersnatch, as someone once said who had seen her from a distance, and take the first turning out of the village which led to the heath. This led through a narrow sandy lane with high, heather-covered banks on each side to one of the valleys, or "bottoms", as they were called locally. At one point, close beside the pathway, stood the homestead of one of the broom-squires, a long, low little house with many outbuildings, and often a pile of heather brooms waiting to be taken to market. A wild-look-ing, hoarsely-barking sheepdog was kennelled near the path in a large beer-barrel turned on its side, and at the sound of a footstep he would leap and bark and rattle his chain like a mad thing. Probably, to some degree, the poor creature *was* mad, for his whole life from puppyhood had been spent on that chain. He was never released even for an hour. What he felt when other, freer dogs gambolled past on their walks with their masters can only be imagined. He had no means of redress in life, poor dog, but in death he had his revenge upon humanity, though not, as so often happens, upon the one who had been responsible for his unnatural existence.

At that time there had been for some weeks an epidemic of dog-poisoning. There were many such barking dogs in the neighbourhood, for at that time and in that district ignorant people thought a watchdog made a better guard if kept constantly on a chain, and one by one they were found in the morning dead before their kennels, poisoned. Great indignation was felt by dog-owners, and it was arranged that a night watch should be kept beside those still living. When it came to our poor friend's turn and the young men,[22] hiding behind a rick, saw a man's form approach in the bright moonlight and place a piece of meat (which afterwards proved to be poisoned) before the dog's kennel, they rushed out from their hiding-place and secured the offender. The dog, meanwhile, snapped up and consumed the meat. The dog died and the men must have had the surprise of their lives when they found they had captured and roughly treated a much respected doctor who had a large house on the border of the heath, a few hundred yards distant from the scene of the crime. He had been running a nursing home for patients with nervous disorders, probably many of them borderline mental cases, for he had male nurses on his staff, and the continual night-and-day barking of suffering dogs had so affected his patients and enraged himself that he had decided to take the extreme measure of poisoning to silence them. He was prosecuted and found guilty, but what legal punishment was meted out to him Laura could not remember though she remembered well that some of the villagers clubbed together to hire a horse brake to take them to witness his trial.[23]

Pity and cowardice combined caused Laura to find a by-pass through a pinewood to avoid what she always thought of as the dog's house, but she could still hear his incessant hoarse barking until she had left the village and its neighbourhood well behind her, and once, when she heard the rattle of a chain among the tree-trunks, her heart stood still, for she thought the dog had broken loose and was about to spring upon her. But the creature that had broken loose and was straying there was only a poor old nanny-goat which, mistaking Laura for its owner, insisted on following her until they came to a stile.

The largest of the green woods was regarded as one of the local beauty spots.[24] It ran for about half a mile along both shores of a

---

[22] James and Henry Belton

[23] Dr Coleclough—fined £10 with £5 costs in May 1900

[24] Waggoners Wells

chain of three small lakes where low-hanging branches dipped down to the water and the pathways were slippery with tree-roots. In spring the green open glades above the lake edges were crowded with the delicate drooping white flowers of the wood anemone, primroses grew in great tufts by the water's brink, and the flowers and budding trees were reflected in the pale green lake water. In autumn the foliage of the trees, red, yellow and russet, was seen in duplicate, above and upon the still, glassy surface where later the many-coloured leaves fallen from the bare branches would float singly and in drifts.

The lakes were one of the sights of the neighbourhood, always visited by strangers staying in the district, and they, with the surrounding woodland, have since been bought by the National Trust.[25] In Laura's time they were a favourite place for picnics, and villagers went there when out for their Sunday evening stroll, but it was seldom that Laura found anyone other than herself there on Sunday mornings. Once, it is true, she disturbed there at his work a photographer who asked her, rather testily, to please move on as he was about to "take a picture". He would, no doubt, have described himself as a photographic -artist, for he evidently took his calling seriously, dressing up to the part in a velveteen jacket and wearing a Vandyke beard. His apparatus consisted of a large wooden camera, the front of which drew out like a concertina, and a heavy wooden tripod. To take his picture he enveloped his head and the back part of his camera in a large square of black velvet.

By one of the paths which led by the lake shores there was at that time a deep sandy basin fed by a spring of crystal clear water which gushed from the bank above. This had been known from time immemorial as the Wishing Well; the local belief was that anyone drinking the water and wishing would have their wish granted, provided they dropped in a pin. In Laura's youth dozens of pins could be seen rusting on the sandy bottom of the well and she dropped in quite a number herself at different times, though what she wished for and whether or not her wishes were granted she could not in old age remember. Twenty years later, when chance brought her to live again in the district, though not at Heatherley, she visited the Wishing Well and found it much altered. A house had been built a few yards from the path and a garden wall stood on the

---

[25] Bought in 1919 and dedicated to the memory of Sir Robert Hunter, a founder of The National Trust who lived locally

bank. The spring water still had an outlet beneath the wall, though it no longer gushed forth in a crystal stream but fell in a thin trickle from a lead pipe, and the deep sandy basin having been filled in, the little stream wandered aimlessly across the path into the green morass on the edge of the wood. Immediately beneath the pipe there was a small puddle, but no pin, rusted or shining new, was to be seen in it, and strange to relate, no-one Laura ever met in the neighbourhood had heard of the Wishing Well. After its centuries of existence, in twenty short years it had disappeared, and the memory of it had faded from men's minds.[26]

Not far from the well there was a deep dingle, closed on three sides by high sandstone cliffs. Ferns and bracken and small scrubby birches filled the greater part of it, primroses bloomed there in the spring and large moist dewberries ripened in autumn. Crowning the tall yellow cliff on one side was a row of tall pine trees. When Laura first knew it, it was a silent, sequestered spot which seldom knew a human footstep. The story went that, eighty or ninety years before, on a dark windy night a horseman who had lost his bearings in the wood had ridden over one of the cliffs and both he and his horse had been killed. The whole countryside had been searched before the broken bodies of horse and rider were found among the bushes and ferns at the bottom of the dell. From that time it had been a place of ill repute. There were people still living who said that, passing nearby on a dark windy night, they had heard the sound of galloping hoofs, and a crash, then silence. When Laura revisited the hollow she found it had been adopted as a dwelling-place by one of the unemployed ex-Servicemen who for a few years after the 1914–1918 war were to be found living in all kinds of odd places. Some of their improvised homes were wretchedly inadequate, a saddening sight, but the occupant of this one called for no pity. He had the cliffs, steep and tall as the sides of a house, to shelter the lean-to of planks in which he slept and the fireplace of bricks in the open which he used for his cooking, and judging by the sizzling sound and the savoury smell, he had bacon and eggs for his supper. He was singing lustily as he turned his rashers that popular song of those years, "The red, red robin keeps bob, bob, bobbing", and he looked pretty bobbish himself. A tinker's outfit on a converted perambulator proclaimed his means of living. If he had a wife or children they were not visible. Probably he had no depend-

---

[26] Since restored

ants, for there was a jolly, carefree ring in his voice and his face was rosy and unlined. He was tidily dressed, quite a presentable fellow in fact, except that he squinted horribly.

He had probably never heard the story of the dead horseman, for the war years had wiped out many such old traditions in country places, and if he had heard it he did not appear to be a man who would, on dark windy nights, hear the soft thud of a horse's foot-falls beneath the trees, followed by the heavy crash of falling bodies, then silence. Horseman and horse had ceased to exist, truly ceased to exist at last. For eighty or ninety years they had survived only in man's memory, from which they had now passed, and the place had become a stage for another scene. Probably today the scene has again changed and has become "that charming wild bit" in some-body's garden.

But on her Sunday morning walks Laura did not often linger by the lakes; she climbed at once by a little sandy track to the heath beyond. It was then, when she felt the heather brush the hem of her skirt and breathed the honey-scented moorland air, that she was filled with a sense of freedom and detachment from ordinary life such as she was never to know elsewhere.

There was one remote part of the heath where the heather had not been cut or burnt as it was cut or burnt periodically in parts nearer the villages. It was tall and thick and shrubby and its long, dark branches almost met over the paths and inlets of cream-col-oured sand. Dotted about it singly were low, stunted-looking trees, some of them with stiff dead branches hung with the smoke-coloured lichen called old-man's beard; a few scattered grey rocks were also lichen-coated, and over the whole scene brooded an air of immense age. As far as the eye could see the activities of man had left no impression. There were no prehistoric earthworks or burial mounds; no flint tools or weapons, such as Laura herself was to find on the heaths nearer the sea in the same county, had ever been found there. There was no squared plot, banked round by turf walls, and no marks of the ploughshare beneath heather or bracken to show, as in other places, that although now deserted, man had had his habit-ation there in times nearer to our own. In its season the heather bloomed purple, then faded through its customary gradations of all shades of pinkish tan to brown and to darkness again, and that was the only visible change in those days; apparently the only one that solitary spot had ever known.

From that high viewpoint Laura would look back on Heatherley and see it as a knot of red roofs, red as a rose against its dark pine trees, and as new to the earth as the rose which had bloomed yesterday, and maybe destined to be almost as fugitive, compared to the continuity of its surroundings. On a morning of April showers and sudden flashes of sunlight she saw the new hotel on the hill beyond Heatherley suddenly stand out from its dark background like a structure carved from ivory. The sun's light had caught its many large windows, which reflected and magnified its beams, and the whole building appeared as though brilliantly illuminated from within. Like a lantern, she thought, like a huge lighted lantern, set down there casually for a moment.

Sometimes she would descend to one of the long, narrow marshes which lay between the hills and explore its pools, standing insecurely on some quaking island of rushes. Newts with smooth dark backs and orange undersides would glide out silently from beneath her feet; frogs squatted sedately, like fat elderly gentlemen, under umbrellas of fern fronds; butterflies hovered in the warm air over the pools, and dragonflies, newly-emerged from their chrysalids, dried their wings and darted away, miracles of blue and silver. In the clearer pools, Laura's own birth plant, Sagittarius, floated its arrow-shaped leaves, and there were other water plants, water-flowers and water-leaves and mosses in abundance. Once she found a few spikes of the bog asphodel, its constellations of yellow starlike blooms shining against the dark rushes, and once, on the heath above, one solitary spike of the rare field gentian, of a heavenly blue. Such were her innocent adventures.

But Laura, though fairly well versed in the ways of the earth, was untrained in the ways of the world. She did and said many things at that time which, to her, seemed natural enough, but which others regarded as doubtful. On the heath, the world forgotten, she was not entirely by the world forgot. Her comings and goings were noted, and those solitary Sunday morning walks were considered by others to be suspicious. One inquisitive person, she was told afterwards, on one occasion took the trouble of following her at a distance, "just to see who she met". His curiosity went unrewarded, but the spying on her movements must to some extent have continued, for her later acquaintance with Bob Pikesley[27] and his sister gave rise to some ill-natured gossip which caused her pain.

---

[27] See Notes at end of book for a possible identity of the Pikesleys

73

She came upon Bob one Sunday morning in one of the more remote parts of the heath which she had but recently discovered, herding his three or four cows which were grazing on one of the natural lawns of rabbit-bitten turf among the gorse bushes. He seemed to her quite an old man. He was short of stature and his slightly hunched shoulders, drooping forward, caused him to appear shorter than he actually was; the skin round his shrewd grey eyes was drawn into wrinkles by his outdoor life, and he wore the earth-coloured garments of poverty on the land. He was never seen without a stick in his hand, a stout, rough ash stick, no doubt of his own cutting, and this he used to flourish at straying cows, to walk with, and in leisure moments to trace patterns of noughts and crosses in the sand. When his cows had found a good pasture he would sit for an hour, hunched up on a bank by the pathway, tracing those curious patterns of his with his stick. He said he could read "at one time", but he had apparently given up reading, perhaps as a bad habit, a waste of time, for at the time Laura knew him he never opened a book and took in no newspaper. Laura at first took him for a labourer, herding the cows of another, but, although he lived the life of a labourer, in all essentials Bob was his own master. He was a small freeholder with commoner's rights and lived in his own cottage with a widowed sister.

Their home was so tucked away between two hills[28] that it was possible to pass within a hundred yards of it without suspecting its existence. It was a narrow thatched cottage with outbuildings in a valley so narrow that their three fields were ribbon-like in length and breadth. As Bob said, you could throw a stone from one hill to another right over the chimney and never know that a house was there. As the hills for the greater part of the day kept out the sunshine theirs was a green garden, a tangle of bushes and ferns and shade-loving plants, such as lily-of-the-valley and Solomon's seal, and the roof of the house was hardly less green than the garden, for houseleek and mosses almost covered the thatch that they could not afford to renew. A little brooklet trickled past the doorway, with beside it a red brick path and the white skeleton of a tree with the branches cut down to form pegs on which to hang the newly-scoured milking pails. The fields got more sunlight than the garden for there the valley became shallower, but the soil was poor and, but

---

[28] Probably in Whitmore Vale

for the grazing on the heath, Bob and his sister could scarcely have made a living.

Morning and evening Bob took his churn of milk in a ramshackle old dairy float drawn by a shaggy heath pony to a dairy in the nearest town and brought back with him such household purchases as were absolutely necessary. When about this business he must have had some converse with his kind, but apparently this did not extend to the discussion of the news of the day, or if it did, he never repeated anything he had heard in the town. All his interest was centred upon his beasts, his poultry and fields, and upon the heath, which he regarded primarily as a storehouse from which he had the right to draw forage and firing. When he had driven his cows out to graze and they had come to a likely pasture, he would sit for hours on some grassy knoll where he could keep watch over them without moving, perhaps without conscious thought.

Whether his remarkable store of heath lore had come from observation or had its source in some instinctive, inborn accumulation of knowledge, was a mystery to Laura. He did not appear to look much about him, in his habitual hunched-up position, his stick either tracing his hieroglyphics on the sand or clasped in his two hands forming a support for his chin, his eyes resting chiefly on the ground. Yet he knew every flower, bird, beast, and reptile upon the heath as well, as he once said in an expansive moment, as the back of his hand. He could in any season, at any spot where he happened to be, lead the way to the nest and exhibit the eggs or the young of any heath-building bird, or point out the place where any desired plant or flower might be found. He could tell the time by the position of the sun and foretell the weather correctly from the wind and clouds.

One day Laura happened to say casually that though she had been told there were adders on the heath she had never seen one. Without saying a word he motioned to her to follow him to a clump of gorse bushes a few yards away where one of the sandy heath paths took a sharp turn. Still without saying anything, he laid his finger on his lips to command silence. A few seconds later a snake thrust its wicked-looking little head from the heather on one side of the path, halted a second to make certain that no danger threatened, then glided across towards the other side. "See them marks?" Bob muttered hoarsely, "them on its neck and back? They're Vs — V's for Viper. Never you touch a snake with them marks on its skin. They're put there to warn folks." Before he had finished speaking the tail of the adder had disappeared into the heather on the other side of the path. Much to Laura's relief, for she had feared she would have to witness the sickening scene of its slaughter. As it was, her spine had gone cold and her flesh all goosey, for she had in full measure the instinctive, unreasoning horror of snakes which seems to be a legacy from the days of the Garden of Eden.

"How did I know 't wer' there?" asked Bob when reseated on his hillock. "Well, I'll tell you; there's no witchcraft about it. While you were talking to me just now, I saw the heather—just over there, see?"—and he pointed, "move in a sort of waves, one behind t'other. You might have thought 't wer' two or three little shrews, or summat, but that 't wer' a snake of some sort, I knew, and as vipers are pretty common hereabouts, being high and dry and hot like, I knew 't wer' likely to be one o' they. Them grass snakes like the cooler places and slow-worms travel so close to the ground they don't make much stir when they move. As to knowing 't would cross that path, any fool could have told that by the direction in which it was going. No, I never trouble to kill the poor things, unless I find one near the cowhouse. They don't hurt me, so why should I go out of my way to hurt them? Besides, I should have my work cut out if I went running with a stick every time I saw a wriggle in the heather."

On another occasion Bob and she had taken cover from a sudden heavy shower in a small pine-clump topping a knoll a few yards from the pathway. Like birds in a cage, Laura thought as she stood watching the long, silver bars of rain streaking down all around, especially as a flock of linnets had also taken refuge there and were flitting and twittering among the upper branches. Bob stood on the outer edge of the little wood keeping watch on his cows and the weather. He had flung the old sack he had brought to sit upon over his shoulders and, leaning forward upon his stick, looked more the old countryman than ever. Presently he straightened himself and looked up at the sky. "'T won't hold up yet a while," he said, "that cloud from the west's getting right overhead. Why don't you sit down and rest yourself?"

Laura looked down at the pine-needles, wet and slippery from previous showers, and shook her head. "Too wet for 'ee?" Bob chuckled, "deary, deary, what a helpless crittur you be. Don't you know that there's always a dry seat under pines in any weather?" And forthwith he stooped and raked aside the top layer of pine-needles and made her feel the warm dryness of those an inch or two beneath. "There!" he said, "just sit down and lean your back against that trunk and you'll have a seat fit for a queen."

But although Bob talked to Laura occasionally, he was by nature a silent man and often their converse was limited to a "good morning" and a few remarks about the weather. Laura, who had an idea that he preferred his own company to hers, would often pass him by at a little distance without speaking. Or she would look down from some hill and see him, sitting in his usual hunched-up position with his eyes on the ground, and wonder what his thoughts were. When she first knew him she thought he might be engrossed in some deep mental speculation. He might be a peasant philosopher or a mute peasant poet with ideas he was unable, or unwilling, to put into words. But that thought, born of her own fancy, was far from the truth. Bob, she found when she knew him better, was a man of limited ideas and as nearly devoid of human feeling as a human being can be. When, very occasionally, he mentioned one of his fellow men he spoke of him gruffly and shortly. Sometimes he would refer casually to his sister. "Jeanette's done this", or "Jeanette says that", but never, as it appeared, with a spark of human feeling.

Once only were his lips unlocked as to any human contact of his, and then a smouldering sense of injustice was responsible for the outburst. Two or three years before Laura came to Heatherley a sanitary inspector, new to the district, had visited Bob's holding to enquire into his dairy methods. He had at once decided that the water supply was inadequate, being at that time obtained from one of the natural valley springs around which the earth had been banked up to form a shallow well. Bob had pleaded that the spring had served his family for their own drinking as well as for dairy purposes for his own lifetime and that of his father before him and that nobody had ever been a ha'porth the worse for the use of it. But his pleading availed nothing; he could not put back the clock; new times had brought new ideas, and what had served in the past could not be permitted to serve a new germ-conscious generation. The ultimatum was that he must either provide a new water supply or sell no more milk.

So a new well had to be sunk at the cost of eighty pounds. If he had possessed that sum or had to borrow it, Bob did not say, but as he accused the inspector of having put him in chains for the rest of his life he probably had to borrow it. Having a load of debt on his shoulders may have accounted for the bitterness of his tone when telling the story of "that dressed up, la-di-da young devil who came from God knows where and went back to the place he belonged to". For the bitter irony of it all to Bob was that the inspector held but a temporary post in the neighbourhood, and before the new well was ready for use he had gone. "Seems he wer' just sent here by the devil or somebody just for the purpose of making me sink that well. Never interfered with nobody else as I ever heard of. I'd well him if I had my way! Put him down a well and make him stay there. But there wouldn't be water in that well. Oh, no! there'd be fire and brimstone."

Laura, as in friendship bound, agreed that it was "hard lines" on Bob that the inspector should ever have come there; but secretly she suspected that the new water supply was necessary, for like others of her generation who read the newspapers, she was acutely germ-conscious.

She only once saw Bob's sister Jeanette. Then Bob had wanted to send her a message and had asked her to call as she passed near the house and deliver it. He asked this simply, not as asking a favour of a grown-up person, but as though speaking to a child. Laura almost expected him to conclude by saying, "you run along quickly now and I'll give you a penny". No penny was mentioned or produced, but she had her reward.

The inside of Bob's house was plain to primitiveness, with a big open fireplace, whitewashed walls, and a brick floor where the feet of passing generations had worn on the soft surface a pathway from doorway to hearth. Of furniture there was but a table and chairs with one corner cupboard from which Jeanette brought forth a glass to fill with milk for Laura. Jeanette looked older than Bob, her hair was quite white while his was brindled; she was tall and upright and had fine dark eyes which, far from being shrewd and even a little cunning, as Bob's were, had a distant, abstracted expression. A listening look, Laura thought, as of one whose ears were astrain to catch some far-away sound. Her accent was better than Bob's and she used no dialect words as he often did, and her clothes, though simple, were neat.

She told Laura that she got up at four o'clock every morning to milk the cows and prepare Bob's breakfast before he left for the town with the milk float. Bob, meanwhile, had the cowshed to clean and his horse to feed and get ready. In addition to these and other regular duties, he would often put in an hour in the fields. When Laura remarked, "It is a hard life for you both", she gave her a quick, penetrating look, as though suddenly aware of her presence, and said, "It might seem so to some people, but there are lives harder." Except for a few commonplace remarks about the weather and the cows, that was almost all the conversation that took place between them, for it was getting late and Laura had to be in punctually for the Sunday dinner. Jeanette did, however, rather to Laura's surprise, ask her to look in and drink a glass of milk whenever she happened to be passing. But Laura never went there again, though at the time she fully intended to do so, for almost immediately afterwards she heard of the gossip about her solitary walks, and curtailed them. She did not give them up entirely, for she could not bring herself to do that, and all the while she remained at Heatherley the heath formed what she felt to be the foundation or background of her life, but thenceforth she walked more circumspectly and more in the beaten track instead of ranging where she would, over the hills and far away.

Twenty years later, when living again in the neighbourhood, she discovered by chance that the woman who came in to clean for her was a native of Heatherley. When asked if she knew Bob and his sister, she said she had known them as children, but later in life they had "turned sort of queer" and nobody had had much to do with them. They were both dead. They had died in that influenza epidemic, as they called it, just after the war. Both down with it at the same time and nobody to look after them. They might easily have died and nobody been any the wiser if the man who had bought their milk had not sent someone to see what had become of Bob and his churns. They took them off to the Cottage Hospital, but it was too late to save them and, in her opinion, hospitals never were much good to those wild kind of people. Look at the gipsies, they always said that to be taken to hospital meant death to one of their tribe.

When gently urged back to the track she said that Jeanette, unlike Bob, had not lived all her life upon the heath. As a girl she had been away in service. Then, for a few years, she had been married to the captain of a small coasting vessel and had accompanied him on his voyages. Mrs Judd said she remembered her coming home for her holidays, "dressed up to the nines" and almost too proud to speak to her old school-fellows. But pride comes before a fall and she had a fall, poor thing, in the long run.

She really did not remember all the ins and outs of what happened, for it was all years ago and she herself at the time had been living up country, married and having an increase every eighteen months, as regular as clockwork. They seemed to manage such things better in these days. But what was she saying, Oh! Yes, well, the husband's ship was wrecked in a storm, off Land's End or somewhere, they were going from Cardiff to London, and Jeanette's husband was drowned and Jeanette herself had some sort of narrow escape. She did remember that much for it was all in the newspapers and someone at home sent her a paper and she read about it. And she thought, though she could not be sure, that Jeanette lost her reason for a time. She was either in an asylum or a hospital, she couldn't say which, and, after all, it didn't much matter. Anyhow, it was a long time before she went back to her old home and then only to wander about the heath like a ghost, never looking at or speaking to anybody. But when her mother got old and ill she seemed to have buckled to again, saw to the house and dairy and nursed her mother through her last illness, and afterwards stayed with her brother. Folks said they were both a bit touched, and she could quite believe it for it would send her stark, staring mad in a month to live out in the wilds as they did.

Poor Jeanette! If that story were true, as no doubt it was in essentials, though vague in the telling, it accounted for the strained, listening expression which had puzzled Laura in girlhood. Above the murmuring of bees in the heath-bells, the soft sighing of pines and the pattering of raindrops, she perhaps sometimes heard the booming of Atlantic rollers above an unmarked grave.

The Hertfords

In some ways Laura had never before been so near happiness as during her first few months at Heatherley. She had work she enjoyed, a new countryside to explore, plenty of books to read, and some interesting people to observe. The one disadvantage was her position as one of the Hertford household. It was distressing to one of her age and disposition to be a silent and uninvolved but embarrassed third when disputes arose between husband and wife, and still more distressing when, as occasionally happened, one or other of the contending couple would appeal to her to bear witness as to some point under dispute. When this happened her usual good sense would desert her and, quite unintentionally, she would say something which would be seized upon by one or the other as supporting evidence on their own side and so add fuel to the flames. Or she would say, often untruthfully, that she did not know, or could not remember what had been said or done a day or two before, which had the effect of offending one or other or both of the disputants.

The brief intervals of reconciliation were almost as trying to witness, the husband's attitude towards his wife being then one of patronising forgiveness and hers towards him one of almost fulsome adoration. Mrs Hertford's attitude towards her husband at such times was sincere, however unwise. In her happier moments she would often declare to Laura that, in spite of his treatment of her, she loved him devotedly. On his side such kindness as he might show towards her appeared to be due to nothing more than a momentary feeling of pity, perhaps of remorse. At other times it was quite obvious to an onlooker that he was only acting a part which happened to suit him at the moment. One evening, on coming into the living-room to bring the office cash for safe keeping during the night, Laura found Mrs Hertford reclining on the hearthrug with her head on her husband's knee, while he, sitting in a low chair, was stroking her hair. The scene, embarrassing enough to one who knew the ordinary relationship of the couple, became for Laura one of horror when the husband, over his devoted wife's head, treated Laura to such a grimace that it sent a cold shiver down her spine.

Then Laura would sometimes wake in the night and hear soft, padding footsteps on the stairs or in the passage outside her bedroom, and more than once or twice she awoke suddenly with the impression that someone had been standing beside her bed. Once she thought she heard the door close softly. She had no key to her door and did not like to ask for one as she was only sleeping there on sufferance and was never sure that she might not have been dreaming; but the idea of that lurking presence by night caused her great uneasiness and she wished that she had some friend, older and wiser than herself, to whom she might go for advice. There was no-one in the village she could confide in without exposing the Hertfords' affairs and it all seemed too indefinite to tell in a letter to her mother. She had not told her anything of the state of unrest in the Hertfords' home for she knew it would worry her, and at that time she had worries enough of her own.

Laura was very much alone in the world at that time. She was far from her home and her childhood's friends and, having but recently arrived at Heatherley, her new friends there were as yet scarcely more than acquaintances. They were, moreover, mostly young people of her own age, pleasant enough to talk to on ordinary subjects, but too unknown and untried for confidences. Nor did she for some time visit her home. Until she had been at Heatherley for a year no holiday was due to her and it was not before her second summer there she could hope to see her family again.[29] And naturally, she could not go to Mrs Hertford with the story of her night fears. She, poor soul, had enough to bear without being troubled by what, after all, might be purely imaginary. By the light of later events she learned that while living under the Hertfords' roof she had been in some personal peril and that her presence there had intensified the strife between the unhappy couple; but of this she had no idea at that time and, no outside accommodation being available, she remained there all through her first winter at Heatherley.

One day in a burst of confidence Mrs Hertford told Laura the story of her marriage. Previously she had been nursery governess to some children whose parents, one summer, had taken a furnished house in the Heatherley district. While there she had met her present husband who had recently undertaken the care of the newly opened post office, which was then a very small one with no telegraph and insufficient other business to require a trained assistant. His housekeeper had so far sold stamps and weighed parcels during the day

---

[29] *In a previous draft to this chapter, she adds here:* She could have gone some months earlier, but she had not her former longing to go home, for her home was no longer what it had been. Her father's weakness for drink had grown upon him and, in consequence, relations between him and her mother were often far from amiable and though, before others, she still stood by him staunchly, hiding his faults and excusing his lapses, the old happy atmosphere had gone. Since leaving their first home where Laura had been born they had lived in three other cottages in the same hamlet, each of them smaller and more inconvenient than the one before, and by that time had come to an anchorage in a very small house on the outskirts of the place, the only advantage of which was that it stood alone, turned its back on its neighbours and looked out over the fields. Her nearly grown-up brother, soon to leave home for many years, was already sleeping downstairs on a made-up bed on the sofa, and when Laura was there either he or she had to sleep at the house of a neighbour. Laura told herself, and almost believed, that there was no place for her at home, yet, when at last she went there, she found the old loving welcome, and the poverty and inconvenience she had shrunk from when at a distance were as nothing compared to the joy of being among her own people. But sufficient reasons remained to forbid her from adding to her own mother's troubles.

and he himself had made up the one bag containing the night mail after working all day at his trade. But the housekeeper was leaving and Mrs Hertford, then Miss Mosley,[30] agreed to take her place. Six months later they were married.[31]

Of what led up to the marriage she gave a probably unintentional hint when she said that there had been gossip about them in the village and that she herself had given notice to leave. He had then asked her to marry him and, at the same time, told her the story of his life which she repeated to Laura. It was the kind of story beloved of minor Victorian novelists and turned upon a father's pride, an obedient daughter's broken heart, and the faithfulness of a lover. Even to Laura, herself a Victorian, it seemed at the time she heard it to belong to some distant period, for by the beginning of this century the old ideas of parental authority and daughterly submission had become greatly modified.

George Hertford had been born the son of an innkeeper, had had a grammar-school education and been apprenticed to what in those days was considered a superior trade, that of cabinetmaker; but when in his late teens he had fallen in love with the daughter of a well-to-do farmer, her parents had forbidden the match as most unsuitable and derogatory. The girl—her name was Letitia, or Letty—must at first have defied her parents to some extent, for George, when telling his future wife the story, had said that it was only by ill usage they had been able to get her to agree to not seeing or writing to him. The form the ill usage took he did not say. They would surely not have used personal violence to their only child, "the apple of their eye", to use George's expression, and it was probably mental, or they may have locked her in her bedroom, though such a measure would be out of date in the eighteen-seventies. At any rate, by some means they prevailed upon her to promise to have no more to do with her lover.

But Letty, although outwardly acquiescing in this arrangement, did contrive to meet George once more and to tell him that her feelings for him were unchanged and unchangeable. They could not elope and get married as they wished, for neither had money, but at that last interview they came to an agreement. George was to emigrate to Australia where men of his trade were said to be making

---

[30] In a previous draft Flora gave her the name 'Miss Covell', then altered it to 'Miss Hidell', and finally to 'Miss Mosley'.

[31] Married at All Saints' Headley, 13th November 1892

fortunes in the large towns. Their plan was that, having saved a sufficient sum from his earnings, he should return to England and claim her hand from her father. The father, they hoped, when convinced of George's improved prospects in life, would consent to their marriage and either take him into partnership on the farm or help him to found a substantial business in his own line as cabinet-maker. If he still withheld his consent to their marriage they would make a runaway match. No letters were to pass between them, Letty was firm on that point for she had given a solemn promise to her parents, but they would hear of each other from time to time through George's parents. In old country fashion they clasped hands over running water and vowed to be true to each other then parted, sadly enough no doubt, but buoyed up by their hopes for the future.

George had booked his passage to Sydney where he had an old workmate who he had hoped would put him in the way of employment, but at Adelaide, where the passengers were permitted to land for a few hours, he was stopped as he left the ship by a stranger who asked him his trade and, when he told him, forthwith offered him employment at high wages. The reports which had reached him in England had not been exaggerated. In the Australian cities there was a great shortage of skilled craftsmen, and cabinet-makers able to make and carve heavy, elaborate pieces of furniture were in special request to meet the demands of those who had made fortunes in gold-mining and were bent upon furnishing their newly-built houses in what they called tiptop style. For three years George, as he said, had only to stoop to pick up money. Laura often heard him tell that part of the story himself and some of his adventures at that time were odd ones. The new millionaires, many of them simple, generous men who had come by their fortunes easily, had, as we should say in these days, money to burn. Not content with paying a high price for an article which pleased them, they would insist as well upon making a handsome present to the workman who had made it. They were fond of large, ornate pieces of furniture, richly carved, and liked to stand by and watch the work in progress. George Hertford had a notable talent for such work and some of his pieces are probably still treasured possessions of antipodean families who point with pride to the interlaced initials of their grandparents, carved by his hand.

From time to time his mother mentioned Letty in her letters. At first there were messages from her, she sent her love and was living for the day of his return. Then the messages became fewer, her parents kept her very close, his mother thought, for she seldom came to the village, but she had seen her in church last Sunday and she had turned round in her seat to smile. She was wearing the sweetest bonnet, kingfisher blue velvet, which suited her fair hair to a T. Her face looked a little peaked and his mother thought she looked thinner, as if she might have been fretting, but nothing for George to worry about; she just mentioned it to let him know that his Letty was not the sort to gad about and make merry during his absence. Then, for one whole summer, Letty was away at the seaside. She had not been very well and the doctor had ordered sea air and sea bathing. But George was not to worry about her, for not much could be wrong; she had had a lovely colour last time his mother had seen her and the sea air[32] would soon set her cough right. Three months later she was back at home, for George's mother had met her in Cudhill Lane and she had sent her love, her dear, dear love, to Georgie. Such meagre news must have been poor fare for a lover, but if it did not satisfy fully, it satisfied the better because the end of his exile was in sight.

He was twenty-two and Letty would be about the same age when, the stipulated sum of money in hand and his passage home already booked, he received a cable from his parents: "Return at once. Letty ill. Her father consents to marriage." It was during the hurry and excitement of the few following days that he had the heat-stroke which so sadly affected his after life. He should have had rest and treatment, but that was impossible, for the ship upon which his passage was booked was about to sail. He got safely on board, then collapsed and lay in his bunk for the greater part of the voyage. By the time he landed in England he had apparently recovered, and had not another and greater shock been awaiting him he might not have felt any serious after-effects.

He had come too late. His father met him at Southampton and somehow and somewhere broke the news to him that Letty was dead. She had died two days before his arrival and he had returned, not to a marriage, but a funeral ceremony. She had never been a robust girl, and after his departure her health had deteriorated. The villagers said that her parents had worried her into her grave by constant reproaches about her engagement, but there was no proof of that and George himself had not believed it after her mother[33] had

---

[32] In a previous draft it is 'Cromer air'

[33] In a previous draft it was her father

told him of her own surprise when Letty, upon what proved to be her deathbed, begged her and her father to send for George. She said Letty had not spoken at home of George for months, and they had concluded that time and absence had done their work and that the memory of her love affair had faded. It may have been so, or it may have been that suppressed grief had hastened, or even caused, her decline. George, of course, believed that she had died for love of him and grieved wildly. During the twenty years which elapsed between Letty's death and his meeting with Mrs Hertford he had twice been back to Australia, drifted from one part of the country to another, and finally, taking the advice of his brother who was in business and doing well there, had settled at Heatherley.

He had probably made some vow to himself never to marry but, as the romantic novelists of that time would have expressed it, to remain true to the memory of his lost love. At any rate, Mrs Hertford told Laura that when he proposed to her—she used the term "proposed"—he told her, "I'll marry you if you will have me, but my heart is buried in poor Letty's grave." "But," she added, when telling the story, "I did not mind that, I felt so sure of winning him over."

That was the story which at the time she first heard it touched Laura to tears. How irrational it sounds in these days and how far away and faded, as faded and out of date as the photograph of the slim, sloping-shouldered girl with a porkpie hat perched on a chignon of fair hair which hung on the wall of Mr Hertford's bedroom. For he had his own bedroom, that was one of the reservations he had made at the time of his marriage, though the arrangement did not appear to interfere with the regular arrival of his children. There were a boy and a girl when Laura first knew them, a girl was born while she was there and two other children after she had left.[34]

As far as Laura was concerned, things came to a climax one night after she had gone to bed and heard a loud bang which she thought at first was some kind of explosion. Rushing out on to the landing she found Mrs Hertford, in her nightdress, coaxing her husband back to bed. He held a small revolver in his hand and Mrs Hertford afterwards told Laura that he had thought he heard whispering beneath the landing window and, thinking it was burglars, he had fired his revolver to scare them away. Whether or not the shot scared anyone below, it certainly scared Laura, and she was

---

[34] See Notes at end of book on Walter Chapman's children

not at all reassured when, thinking the proper time had come to tell Mrs Hertford about the footsteps she thought she had heard at night and of her impression that someone had been in her room, she was told that it was one of Mr Hertford's habits to prowl about the house at all hours of the night, opening and shutting doors and looking into dark corners with the idea of finding some unnamed enemy he believed was lying in wait for him. He had sometimes been in Laura's room at night for it was one of his ideas that Laura might be in league with the enemy. When he had this idea he would call his wife up from her sleep to play propriety, and while she stood at the door, he, with a shaded candle in his hand, would creep softly into the room to see if anyone beside Laura was there. Laura, of course, was always alone and in bed with her hair screwed up in Hind's curlers and her face thickly cold-creamed, and so obviously asleep that, for a time, he was pacified. At other times it was his wife he suspected, or her and Laura in collusion, and he even accused his little children of carrying messages from one to the other. The reason for this strange behaviour was that the poor man's mind was affected. His wife must already have had some suspicion of this, for she told Laura that she had begged him, time after time, to consult a doctor about the violent headaches from which he suffered; but the mere mention of seeing a doctor threw him into one of his rages and she dared not herself take steps to have him medically examined. A few years later he totally lost his reason and ended his days in Broadmoor Criminal Asylum.[35]

After that night of terror Laura felt that she could not remain under that roof a day longer than was absolutely necessary and made such a determined effort to find herself a room outside that, in less than a week, she had removed herself and her belongings from the house. Not without an uneasy feeling that she was deserting Mrs Hertford, who, however, seemed rather relieved than otherwise when told of the new arrangement. Her husband, she said, was always at his worst when anyone outside his own family was present. Their most innocent actions provoked his suspicions and the effort to find out where they were and what they were doing kept him in a constant state of excitement. Alone, she said, she could manage him better.

Before Laura left, Mrs Hertford adjured her solemnly not to say a word to any living creature about anything she had seen or heard

---

[35] He died on 15th September 1921

while living with them. She promised willingly and kept her promise, and as far as she ever heard, no-one in the village, with the exception of herself and Alma, had any idea that the relationship between the postmaster and his wife was other than normal. Then, gradually, as Laura came to see less of the Hertfords' home life and her own outside interests increased, their affairs no longer troubled her to the extent they had done. Sometimes, indeed, seeing Mr Hertford stand, calm and collected, coolly discussing some trade order with a customer and drawing little pencil sketches to illustrate his suggestions, she felt that she must have imagined that pistol-shot. But there were other times when, sitting at the telegraph instrument, she heard the old sounds of strife within doors, or when some confidence of Mrs Hertford's would bring to her mind the old fears and misgivings and she felt she was treading on treacherous ground. During the whole of her time at Heatherley, even in moments of personal happiness, she was aware, if but dimly, of a sinister cloud in the background.

As may be imagined, it was not easy to find a cheap lodging in a place where cottage front rooms could be let for a couple of guineas a week in the season. For a few weeks Laura lived as a boarder with a retired business couple and their grown-up daughter in one of the villas just beyond the village street. There she had a bedroom with the whitest of stiffly starched counterpanes on the bed, framed texts upon the walls and a looking-glass draped with lace and blue ribbon; plenty of good, solid food, her laundry done for her free of charge and even her stockings mended, for the inclusive charge of ten shillings weekly. One thing only was denied her; there was not a shred of privacy. If she came downstairs dressed to go out she was expected to say where she was going and why, and, if for a walk, she was bidden to wait "just a tick" while Clara got ready to accompany her. "I know she'd like a walk," her mother would say, "for she said just now she wouldn't mind one, only, of course, she'd got nobody to go out with," and Clara would come sailing downstairs in her fine clothes and high-heeled town shoes and the two would saunter along the main road, stopping to hold long conversations with anyone who was known to Clara. If Laura went to her bedroom to write a letter or to read she was seldom there more than ten minutes before there would come a tap at the door and a cheerful voice outside would call out: "Whatever are you doing up here by yourself? There's a fire in the parlour and Clara's just going to try over her new piece on the piano and she wants you to come down and hear it", and if that invitation failed to allure, Clara's own refined Cockney accent would be heard on the stairs, calling: "Come down, you poor lonely little thing, and let's cheer you up a bit!" Laura felt bound to comply for she knew such invitations were kindly meant, but for her, the walk was ruined and the evening downstairs not only wasted, but unutterably boring.

Though kind-hearted, Mrs Binks had not much delicacy of feeling. She several times pointed out to Laura what a great advantage it was to be permitted to share such a home as theirs, and for such a small sum weekly. "But," she would add, "we can well afford to take you at that price and we like having you, reely, for you're company for Clara and it's been dull for her since we retired and came to live in the country. In London, of course, she had troops of pals, she was the life and soul of the company wherever she went, but here, the people are either stuck up or such as we couldn't let her associate with, so we thought if we could get a business girl such as yourself of about her own age she'd feel more happy and settled like." So, Laura noted, she had been taken in as a companion for Clara, and being companion to Clara was not a position she enjoyed, for although Clara was all very well in her way, her way was not Laura's way and she had no wish to be forced into it. Yet they were all so well-meaning and kindly disposed that when she heard of a room such as she had really wanted she was hard put to it to find an excuse for leaving them. Mrs Binks begged her to say if there was anything she did not like in their arrangements, "because, you know, if there's anything different you'd fancy to eat we could get that for you, and if you'd like your breakfast a mite earlier, and I know you've had to run for it at times, I'll make that girl put on the kettle before she takes off her hat in the morning and you shall have your breakfast without waiting for us, for as you know, we're none of us very early risers." Laura caught at the idea of having to start work early and said she wanted to live nearer the post office, which reason for leaving could not have been very convincing, coming from one who made nothing of a ten-mile walk, but it served, although there was ever after a pained, disappointed-in-you expression on each of their three faces whenever she happened to meet them.

Living alone and liking it

Laura never forgot the feeling of exaltation she experienced when, her day's work done, she for the first time approached her new dwelling, saw the flicker of firelight on an upper window and knew the room in which the fire had been lighted was *her* room, in which she could shut herself up without fear of intrusion. After she had had her evening meal and arranged her few possessions she sat on, long after her usual bedtime, enjoying her first taste of freedom for months. It was a wild March night with the wind blustering round the outside walls of the house and rattling the none-too-well-fitting windows, and as long as the fire lasted puffs of smoke came down the chimney into her face; but far from causing her any discomfort the storm made her situation more pleasing for, in contrast with the outer world, her room seemed to her a little haven of peace.

The house had been built by a speculating builder with the idea of attracting a superior type of purchaser or tenant; but as it had a very small garden and was closely neighboured by a group of poor cottages, he had for some time been unable either to sell or let it. It had then been let to two working-class families, one occupying the rooms on one side of the house and the other those on the other side, and with one of these it had been agreed that Laura should rent their front room upstairs. It was a fair sized room with two windows, one of them with a view of the heath with, in the distance, the long wavy line of blue hills she had seen on the day she reached Heatherley.

The room was but poorly furnished and its two or three thread-bare rugs were islands in a broad expanse of scrubbed boards; but it was clean and cheap at the rent of four shillings a week, which included some attendance. It would probably have been let to summer visitors had the landlady possessed better furniture and a smaller family of her own to attend to, but as that was out of the question—for what well-paying visitor would have tolerated uncarpeted stairs which children of two families used as a play-ground, or patched sheets and hastily prepared meals?—it was reserved for "a young person in business. Out all day preferred", and, for more than two years, that young person was Laura.

It would be possible to write a pathetic account of Laura's life at that time with its long working hours, poorly furnished bed-sitting room, scrappy meals, absence of opportunity for organised recreation, inferior social status. But though correct in the main as to facts, such an account would not be true to life, not to Laura's life at any rate. The bare room did not strike her as particularly bare: it had a clean bed, a table, primarily for meals, at which she could write, shelves in a recess by the fireplace for her books, a shabby but comfortable old easy-chair, patched on both elbows, and a paraffin lamp which her landlady had bought at an auction sale. Laura thought the lamp, when lighted, gave quite an air to the room with its red, crinkled silk shade and embossed figures on its silver-coloured base. It certainly smelt a little, but when she remarked upon this her landlady told her that she used for it only the best tea-rose lamp-oil and, after that, the name of the brand of oil seemed to sweeten the scent.

A friend who once called to see Laura told her that she should go "balmy on the crumpet" sitting up there with nobody to talk to, but the quiet and solitude which would have been poison to Kitty were spiritual meat and drink to Laura. As to poverty, she had been born to that, and to her social inferiority she gave no thought, for already, as in after life, it was to her the individual who counted, not his or her place in society. Though not what is now called "a good mixer" in general assemblies, she was in the course of her life to find friends in all classes except the most exalted and the most depressed, and might possibly have found them at both of those extremes had opportunity offered.

As Laura's salary was but one pound weekly she had, after her rent was paid, to keep down her living expenses, including laundry and coals in winter, to ten shillings a week, and it may be of interest to hear of the prices which made this possible. The South African war, already in progress, was to send prices up to a level from which they would never descend but, on the contrary, rise to what were then almost unbelievable heights as the years went on. Already, before the war had affected them, food and other commodities were much dearer than in Laura's childhood. A pint of new milk cost three halfpence, fresh farm butter from a shilling to one-and-four a pound, new-laid eggs from tenpence to one-and-two a dozen according to season. The best back rashers of Hampshire bacon cost eightpence a pound, a small lamb chop or cutlet four-pence or fivepence, and a small dab or plaice about the same amount.

As long as no-one but herself was qualified to work the telegraph instrument, Laura was unable to leave the office for her midday meal and, for a time, had fetched for her by a telegraph messenger one of the ninepenny dinners which were a feature of the new model inn.[36] It was an immense nine-pennyworth and included a thick cut off the joint, two or more vegetables, and a wedge of fruit tart or a round of roly-poly, sufficient for three dinners for one with her appetite. Mrs Hertford kindly stored and heated up for the next day what was left, but Laura soon tired of such heavy and monotonous food and preferred to bring with her bread and cheese and an apple, or to send out for a glass of milk and a bun, and to wait for a more substantial meal until she reached home in the evening.

After the inn dinners were discontinued the foundation of her diet was a pint of milk daily, and weekly a half-pound of farm

---

[36] *Fox & Pelican*, Grayshott, opened in August 1899 by the Bishop of Winchester's wife

butter and a dozen new-laid eggs. These were local produce brought round on a donkey-cart by an old countrywoman known as Mammy Pasfield who wore a big white apron and a sunbonnet. She was a kind old soul who always apologised for what she considered the high price she had to ask for her produce, and to salve her own conscience and to please her customer, always threw something in— an apple or a bunch of flowers, and once an immense savoy cabbage.

Laura's chief meal of the day was what is, or was, known in Scotland as tea with an egg to it. Sometimes, by way of variety, she would have her egg fried with a rasher, or a little fish or a tiny chop, with plenty of bread but no vegetables, not even potatoes, because it was not in the bond that her landlady should cook for her what she called a full meal. She was supposed to get her dinner out. And no jam, cakes, or pastry because Laura did not care for sweet foods. She ate a good many apples and other fruit when obtainable. Upon this diet she lived in the best of good health for two years and a half and indeed, although there were some deficiencies according to modern scientific ideas, she had most of the foods regarded today as essential to healthy living. She had not as yet become a cigarette smoker, but had she been, a packet of five woodbines would have cost but one penny. One of the saddest features of later life is the knowledge of such lost opportunities!

Clothing was more of a problem than food. In those days there were no attractive little ready-made frocks to be bought for a few shillings. Ready-made frocks were certainly obtainable, but they fell into one or other of two categories—what the shopkeepers called models on the one hand, and on the other the cheap and nasty—and Laura, who was not at all handy with her needle, had to pay a dressmaker to make her frocks, and consequently they were too expensive to have more than one a year. Cotton blouses and serge skirts were her ordinary office wear; the blouses made with stiff, stand-up collars and worn with a tie. In this attire she flattered herself that she looked very neat and businesslike, but she often longed for something softer to the touch and more becoming. Her hair she wore twisted into what was known as a teapot-handle high up on the back of her head, with a heavy curled fringe on her fore- head; topped, when she left the office at night, with one of the stiff round white straw hats known as sailors, which for several years were the universal everyday wear of women of all classes. But even this fashion in sailor hats did not remain static. One year there would be broader or narrower brims than the last or the crown would be higher or lower, and the angle at which the hat was worn varied from year to year. At one time it was worn tilted over the nose of the wearer, at another it had slipped down to the back of the head and formed a kind of halo. Unbelievable as it may appear, the sailor hat, with its stiff outline softened by the curls on the forehead, was not at all an unbecoming fashion to most women and another recommendation was that a good quality sailor hat could be bought for two shillings; an inferior copy cost eightpence.

For better wear, before she went to Heatherley, Laura in a reckless hour had had a grey coat and skirt made for her by a tailor, for which she had paid two guineas in instalments, and a kind aunt had by a coincidence sent her for a birthday present a perfectly toning muff and fur necklet of the then fashionable grey, silky, thickly-curling fur called Thibet. These, with a white muslin frock for hot Sundays, or a white blouse worn with a white piqué skirt, served her all the time she was there. Her best hat in winter was a close-fitting affair puckered up by herself from a square of black velvet; in summer, a large, floppy white straw trimmed by herself with a wreath of artificial roses which figured on hat after hat. Shoes and shoe-mending, stockings and underwear, soap and tooth powder, writing and sewing materials and an occasional book had to be contrived from an income of one pound a week.

Nothing was spent on amusements. There were no amusements to spend money on, except, once a year, the one-shilling entrance fee to the parish social evening, by that time known as a *soirée.* This was held in a neighbouring settlement in a newly-built hall belonging to a religious denomination which, when not using it for its own purposes, was willing to let it for any public event.[37] In that hall Laura several times heard Mr Bernard Shaw lecture on Socialism. He was freely interrupted and questioned by his audience, to which at that time the initials G.B.S. had no special significance. On one occasion a working man stood up in the body of the hall to argue some point with the lecturer and, being absolutely unselfconscious and unimpressed by a reputation of which he knew nothing, acquitted himself very creditably. On another occasion an elderly reporter on one of the local newspapers engaged in a long and heated contest with the same distinguished lecturer about unearned increment; but as the term was new to him and he had failed to grasp its exact

---

[37] Congregational Hall, Hindhead, opened 1896

meaning, the debate ended with his collapse and apology. Other speakers expounded their views on Spiritualism, Vegetarianism, Unrest in the Balkans, different aspects of the Boer War, the duties and limitations of womanhood and other subjects.

Laura also attended one of a series of readings of their own work by living writers. That evening Ian Maclaren, the Scottish novelist, read from his then very popular book, *Beside the Bonny Briar Bush*. More exciting was the occasion when a travelling troupe of actors in Elizabethan dress entertained the company with hand-bell ringing and Elizabethan part-songs, with quips and anecdotes by the leader, who also sang as solos most of the songs from the plays of Shakespeare. It was a simple enough performance but there was something about those who took part in it, especially about the leader, which gave an almost perfect illusion of Elizabethan reality. There was gusto and such an apparent joy in life that, together with the period dress and a remarkable resemblance in the features of the leader to Shakespeare himself, gave at least one of the audience the sensation of having been magically wafted back three centuries in time to Elizabethan London. Laura never heard the cognomen of the troupe or the name of its leader, nor did anyone else in the audience ever mention the performance to her afterwards; but to her, for life, the memory of it remained not as an entertainment but as a magic glimpse of the past.

Then later, the famous Cappers came to the hall and read everyone's most secret thoughts, after they had been written down and the paper folded. Or husband and wife would retire from the hall, come back blindfolded and discover some small article concealed during their absence. It was a clever display. The written, but concealed, thoughts were with one or two exceptions more or less accurately deciphered and the hidden articles found, but there was an expression of great strain and tension on the faces and in the movements of the thought-readers, who seemed to divine at too great a cost of physical and mental effort such questions as "Wonder what I'll get for my supper?"; and the husband, led by his wife by the hand, straining like a hunting dog on the leash, should have had something more important to find than a thimble or a matchbox. Still, the Cappers were all the rage in London at that time and it was something for country mice to be able to say that they had seen them, especially for those who had had their thoughts read by them.

As the hall belonged to a religious body it was not available for dancing. But the new dancing era had begun; there was in the parish a large wooden hut which had once been used as a temporary church, and there cheap, popular dances took place whenever anyone could be found to organise them. There were also public dances in a large room over one of the inns which were well attended by the young people of the village. These were not the old, informal country dances of Laura's childhood, but more sophisticated affairs; there was a Master of Ceremonies, a piano and a violin to play up-to-date waltzes, and most of the girls and young women who attended made some attempt at evening dress.

As Laura had no latchkey, when she took part in any such evening diversions her landlady or her husband would sit up for her, and when she came in, say at eleven, their tired faces would silently reproach her for keeping late hours. She knew better what was expected of her than to stay out after ten on ordinary evenings. On one of the very few occasions when she transgressed this unwritten law, although she was barely a quarter past the hour, she was received with cold looks and sundry hints as to what was and was not becoming in an unmarried girl.

That evening she had had one of those small curious experiences which, though nothing much in themselves, seem to us afterwards to have a hidden significance. It had been a lovely May day and when she left the office and breathed the soft, lilac-scented air and saw all the signs of spring around her she had felt the folly of going immediately indoors. It was the season of nightingale song, and as this was never heard close around Heatherley, perhaps because most of the trees were pine trees, she thought she would walk a mile or two out on the main road to one of the known haunts of the bird. She had not gone more than a mile when, coming to a bend in the road, she saw before her a thicket of tall old thorn trees in full bloom. Sheeted in snowy blossom, they stood in a semi-circle on the edge of the heath and she turned aside and stood for a long time among them, looking up through their glimmering branches at the stars twinkling out, one by one, in the grey-blue twilight. Petals drifted down on her face, light as snowflakes, and the air was faintly sweet with the scent of the may. Although but a few yards away from one of the main arteries of traffic to the coast, the spot was at that hour deserted and the silence profound. She heard no nightingales. It was evidently not one of their concert nights, or perhaps the sight of the blossoming may and nightingale song together would be too much of beauty to be vouchsafed to one poor mortal.

She heard no nightingales, but while standing there, concealed in the shadow of the trees, she heard, approaching her on the road, the soft, slithering sound of deflated bicycle tyres. The bicycle and its rider came slowly into her view, still with that heavy, slithering sound, and she saw in the dusk the silhouette of an ordinary sailor on the saddle, an ordinary bell-bottomed bluejacket. But his behaviour was not at all ordinary for, leaning forward over the handlebars, he was sobbing brokenheartedly. He approached and passed her, unaware of her existence, and she, knowing nothing of the cause of his grief, grieved with and for him as she came out of her hiding-place and walked soberly home. She had gone out to hear nightingales and heard instead the desolate sound of human suffering, and that against a background of pure loveliness.

When Laura first went to live in her house her landlady, Mrs Parkhurst,[38] was about forty-five, a tall, massively built woman with dark hair and eyes and well-defined features. Occasionally, when some passing excitement brought a faint flush to her sallow cheeks and caused her dark eyes to kindle, she might still have been thought a handsome woman, but constant childbearing and the strain of bringing up a large family on insufficient means had lined her face, sharpened her voice, and destroyed the contours of her figure. In her person she was scrupulously clean and fairly tidy. Her dress was that of all overworked working-class mothers of that day, patched and faded old garments of nondescript hue partly covered by a large white apron.

She had seven children still living at home, and with washing and ironing and cleaning and cooking for ten people her life was a hard one. At an hour when more privileged housewives were enjoying their evening amusement or evening repose she was cooking a hot meal for her husband and two sons who had been away at work all day and she had yet to wash up, pack their meals for the morrow, get her younger children to bed and do what was necessary for Laura. Sometimes, when asked if she did not feel tired, she would say: "I do. I don't believe I've sat down a moment all day, except to meals."

The couple who rented the other part of the house had three small children, and with those and Mrs Parkhurst's own three little girls running in and out, or playing in the hall or on the stairs in wet weather, the view of the interior of the house from the front doorstep

---

[38] Called 'Mrs Chivers' in a previous draft

was often far from attractive. The stairs being used in common by both families, neither housewife felt inclined to provide a stair-covering, and the bare boards, though frequently scrubbed, gave the place a poverty-stricken appearance to those who came no farther than the front door. That entrance was perhaps one of the reasons why Mrs Parkhurst's reputation was not as good as it should have been with district visitors and other kind ladies who visited the poor in their own homes. One of them once commiserated with Laura for being obliged to live in such a poor lodging. For they felt it their duty to keep an eye on Laura too, though their good intentions towards her were fruitless. They had parties and dancing classes for their own young people and ran a club with a gymnasium for those they called working girls, chiefly for those working in a large steam laundry in the district; but for neither group was Laura qualified. She did not seem to fit in anywhere, as one lady regretfully told her. A state of things Laura acknowledged with alacrity.

Apparently Mrs Parkhurst did not fit in either. She had no time to attend Mothers' Meetings, even had she wished to do so, and indeed was not even a churchgoer, so all they could do was to bring her a copy of the Parish Magazine, spy out the land while inquiring about the health of her family, and go away shaking their heads. None of them liked her; she was too independent and forthright in her manner to please their taste, and calling as they did at odd hours and seeing her browsed from housework, they put her down as a slattern. Yet Mrs Parkhurst did not strike Laura as a common woman. Her height and bearing may have had something to do with that impression, but there was something more—a core of integrity, of good breeding, a positive note of personality—which distinguished her from the mass of humanity.

With so much to occupy and harass her, her voice was sometimes raised in anger, and that, as she herself said, was bound to be just as one of the visiting ladies came knocking at the door. But, even in anger, she never attacked the offender by making the wildly exaggerated charges or by using the threats and expressions which, though meaningless and generally understood as being so, made hideous the domestic life of some such families. Her ordinary manner towards her children was kind and motherly. She appeared to understand and to make allowance for their varying dispositions; was not too hard on her elder boys when they stayed out late in the evening, and bore patiently such trials, caused by the younger children, as broken crockery, torn clothing, and muddied floors.

Her husband was a tired-looking, ageing man, smaller and weaker physically than herself and inferior in type. As a wage-earner he was a hardworking and trustworthy man, though not a skilled one, and they counted as one of their chief blessings that he had not been unemployed for a day since they married. Mrs Parkhurst loyally held him up to her children as the head of the household. "We must ask your father", she would say, or "We'll see what your Dad says about it"; but, in fact, she was in every way the leading spirit and shouldered his share of responsibility as well as her own simply and naturally. He, for his part, was well contented that it should be so and regarded her with the same loving admiration, mixed with tolerance of "her little ways", as that shown by her grown-up sons.

The Parkhursts belonged to an obscure dissenting sect which had no meeting place nearer than that in a market town seven miles distant.[39] As there was no public conveyance between there and Heatherley, Mrs Parkhurst and her younger children were unable to attend the services. Her elder boys had no wish to attend; one of them went to church with his girl, the others had their own ways of spending the Sabbath, and it was left to Mr Parkhurst to represent the entire family. Once a month, early on Sunday morning, he would come downstairs, dressed in his best and newly shaved, and set out on his long walk with a packet of bread and cheese in his pocket to eat between services, if none of the brethren invited him to dinner. More often than not he received such an invitation, for, though all of them poor, they appeared to live up to their watchword, "Let brotherly love continue"; but there were occasions when no one thought of him and he stole away by himself to eat his humble provender. Those were known in the family as "Dad's chapel Sundays", and on those days, after the huge Sunday dinner had been eaten and the washing-up done, Mrs Parkhurst would dress herself more carefully than on ordinary Sundays, gather round her her younger children and read to them from a monthly tract she received called *The Young Believer*. The children would probably have been better taught at the church Sunday School, and she would certainly have been more in favour with the visiting ladies had she sent them there, but such was her idea of her duty to her children, and she carried it out to the best of her ability.

---

[39] Godalming and Farnham are seven miles distant, and Petersfield (the most likely location) about ten miles

As far as Laura could judge from what she heard, the tenets of their sect were harsh and narrow. Theatre-going, dancing, and novel-reading were counted as sins and those who indulged in those pastimes were bound for perdition. Laura's own diversions must often have shocked her kindly landlady, though she never openly censured them. Perhaps she regarded them as she did those of another person of whom she once said with a sigh: "Well, we can only pray for him." But the way of the congregation was not too strait to leave room for warm human feeling. On one occasion Laura happened to be present when Mr Parkhurst returned from chapel with the news that one of the sisterhood had died, evidently one who had taken a prominent part in the life of the community, for, after a moment of shocked silence, Mrs Parkhurst exclaimed: "Oh, she'll be missed! She'll be missed sorely! Who's going to take the Women's Bible Readings, and look after the sick and the out of works in winter and see that the rent of the chapel is paid! Whoever does it, and the Lord'll raise up some friend, we shall never see her like again. She was a Mother in Israel! A real Mother in Israel!"

Twice a year the minister of the denomination cycled over to pay Mrs Parkhurst a pastoral visit. With commendable delicacy he always let her know beforehand when to expect him, and, in consequence, found Mrs Parkhurst dressed in her best, the parlour swept and garnished and a suitable tea prepared. After one of his visits, when Laura came home in the evening, she found Mrs Parkhurst in a cheerful, almost exalted mood. "I've had a blessed time," she said, "a truly blessed time, and I feel a new creature for it!" After another of Mr Lupton's visits, Laura said she hoped the children had been good and not bothered her by running in and out of the room. She said they had been good enough, and well they might be, for Mr Lupton had insisted upon having them in to share with him the dish of small cakes she had made specially for his tea. Afterwards he had told them about Our Lord when He said "Suffer little children to come unto me"; then he had laid his own hand on their heads and blessed them and sent them back to their play.

With so much to do for her own numerous family Mrs Parkhurst had little time to devote to her lodger, but she did faithfully all she had undertaken to do, and a little more. The fires she lighted always burned up brightly, the meal she had cooked was served to time, and often, as a freewill offering, there would be on the table a few flowers of her own growing or a freshly baked scone or bun. Sometimes, when she knew Mrs Parkhurst had had a hard day at the washtub, Laura would have liked to relieve her by lighting her own fire and getting her own meal, but she had by that time gained enough knowledge of the world to know that for her to go in and out of the kitchen at odd times would either be looked upon as an intrusion or, on the other hand, that it would soon lead to her being expected to take her meals there as one of the family. So she did what she could to help by getting up early enough to make her own bed and leave the room tidy, and by doing any oddments of shopping to save Mrs Parkhurst the walk to the village, so that Mrs Parkhurst, who hitherto had had only young men lodgers, was pleased with what she called a helping hand.

But Mrs Parkhurst was no saint; she could, at times, be very irritating. She was not an intrusive or a talkative woman and did not pry unduly into Laura's affairs, but their respective ages and their position as landlady and lodger gave her, as she thought, some right of censorship. When she did not approve of Laura's proceedings she would be more than habitually reserved, or she would throw out hints, ostensibly general hints, as to her own standard of behaviour for young women living away from home. She did not, for instance, believe in such young persons having friends of the opposite sex; or, if they had one such friend, he must be the only one. Of girls who were seen home from an entertainment by one young man one week and the following week by another she did not approve, and when Laura suggested that there was safety in numbers, she told her she was one of those who go round and round the wood and bring out a crooked stick in the end.

Her ideas on dress differed greatly from Laura's. She did not presume to criticise openly any of Laura's belongings, but seeing her attired for some special festival in white muslin and a rose-wreathed hat she would remark, somewhat sourly, that in her opinion nothing was more becoming to a girl than a neat costume and sailor hat. She could go anywhere in that dress and be respected, for it always looked good. She never had held with a lot of finery. This was vexing to a girl who had thought she looked both suitably and becomingly dressed for a fête where there was to be outdoor dancing. On the subject of dancing she was surprisingly broadminded. To her and her co-religionists dancing was a sin, but she admitted that she knew that many truly Christian people saw no harm in it.

When she approved of Laura's behaviour she would signify her approval by a warmer welcome than usual, or by some small act of kindness such as washing for her, free of cost, some article of apparel. At such times, if she had a few spare moments, she would stay for a chat when she cleared away the tea things, and in that way Laura came to know something of her life.

She had been born and lived as a child in a hamlet near Selborne, Gilbert White's Selborne, and was proud of her birth-place. "You should see the Hanger at Selborne", she would say when Laura brought in wild flowers. "You should see it in spring, when the primroses are out, you could sit down and pick your hat full without moving." Her father had owned or rented a little land and they had kept fowls, geese, and a pig or two, and he had, in addition to his work at home, put in a day here and there working for wages. Every year at the beginning of the hop-picking season the whole family had been packed, bag and baggage, into a little donkey-cart they had and had gone to work in some hop-gardens near Farnham, leaving only the old grandmother at home to keep house and attend to the animals.

She looked back on those hop-picking days as the happiest of her life; "'Twas a regular holiday for us children," she declared, "though every one of us big enough to stand on our two legs had to work hard. But if we worked all day we had plenty of fun playing round the fire with the other children in the evening while our mums cooked our suppers and washed our clothes, and a fine hearty appetite we had all of us, for the smell of the hops was as good as a medicine. 'I'm that hungry I could eat a child dead of the smallpox', our dad used to say, but that was only his fun, you know. He liked good food and he got it when hopping, great big stews cooked in a three-legged pot slung over the fire, with young rabbits and mush-rooms and a nice bit of bacon we'd brought with us from home, and the men clubbed together to buy a barrel of beer for themselves and, after supper, they'd all sit round the fires and sing. Everybody in the villages round went hopping in those days. The farmers gave as many men as they could spare a holiday and the few left at home did for themselves while their wives and children were away. The houses were all shut up in the daytime and not a soul to be seen in the place, excepting a few old grannies left behind to feed the cats and the pigs and so on. Now, of course, there's all this riff-raff from towns in the hop-gardens and nobody who thinks themselves respectable goes any more; but then it was a holiday for the whole countryside. And when settling-up time came there was a present for every one of us children. 'Twas supposed to be a prize for those who worked hardest, but though. some worked harder than others, as is but human nature, nobody was ever left out that I can remember. My father bought me a doll one year, and a beautiful doll it was, that opened and shut its eyes and squeaked when you pressed a spring in its chest. I wish I could give a doll like that to our young Ivy, but times have changed and such a doll would cost nine or ten shillings now; and there's no chance of going hopping either, as a man who works for wages in these days can't take a fortnight or three weeks off to go hopping or somebody else would soon be stepping into his shoes on his job. Then the farmers were glad to let men off after the harvest was carried. It saved them paying out wages when there was nothing much doing for a week or two. The gipsies do a lot of it now, them and that rough lot from towns, and the hop-gardens aren't what they were when everybody under gentry thought it no come-down to lend a hand with the picking."

When Laura asked if she had in her childhood heard of an old-time curate[40] of Selborne who had written a book about birds, she said she thought she had heard the name of Gilbert White mentioned at some time, but she was not sure. Which was disappointing to Laura, who had hoped to glean some local traditions of the celebrated parson-naturalist. But although disappointed she was not surprised, for even in her own time, thirty years later than that of Mrs Parkhurst, not much attention was given to local history in elementary schools. One of her own regrets in later life was that in her childhood she had not known that the poet Pope had visited the local mansion near her home and had actually written part or the whole of *The Rape of the Lock* there. When she learned this in middle life she had long left her old home and had little prospect of seeing it again, and though she was still able to picture the frail, crooked little figure in a black cloak pacing the beech avenue which had been her own favourite haunt as a child, age and distance took off the edge of the delight she would have experienced had she known that she was treading in the footsteps of a real poet.

Laura thought of the Parkhursts as elderly people. Their eldest son was the same age as herself; they had a daughter away in service, who was soon to be married; and they often spoke of themselves as getting on in years and said that, as the younger children grew up, they hoped for an easier time for themselves. That hope

----

[40] Flora actually wrote 'rector'—but Margaret Lane corrected this to 'curate'

was not soon to be realised. At the age of forty-seven and while Laura was still living with them Mrs Parkhurst once more found herself pregnant. It was a difficult position for her, surrounded by her grown and growing-up family, and she had physically a miserable time in the early months. Her face grew yellow and thin and the hitherto faint lines became wrinkles; but only once did Laura know her to make anything approaching a complaint. Then she had been speaking of babies' clothes and had said that all she had were worn out or had been given away long before, and how to get new ones she did not know. "I did think I had done with all that", she said, and tears welled into her eyes as she said it. She wiped them away with a corner of her apron and added: "But I know it is God's will and I must be patient, though I do dread the time when it begins showing."

When the time came she had a long and difficult confinement, with two doctors in attendance. The district nurse told Laura afterwards that her fortitude was wonderful. "And what do you think she said when she came round from the chloroform? You'd never guess in a month of Sundays. 'I know that my Redeemer liveth!' says she, 'I know that my Redeemer liveth.' I didn't know she was a religious woman, did you?"

A few days later Laura said good-bye to Mrs Parkhurst, as she thought then for ever. She was resting peacefully in bed with her youngest daughter on her arm and her eldest, aged twenty, in attendance as nurse. She said it was the first good rest she had had since Ivy was born and she meant to make the most of it. "You'd better! for it's the last you'll get of this sort, my lady!" laughed her grown-up daughter who, in view of her new responsibilities and her own approaching marriage, was indulging in the airs of mature womanhood. She took the gurgling morsel of humanity from the bed and, patting it vigorously on the back, assured it that it should have its nicey-picey dilly-dilly-dilly-water in a little min-min, when brother Herbie came back from the chemie's, and that nursey-pursey would soon be coming to give baby its bathie-pathie, while her mother looked proudly on, exclaiming "How natural it all comes to her!" The old freemasonry of sex was working. Mrs Parkhurst's husband had gone out that morning looking as if the cares of the whole world had suddenly rolled from his shoulders. A plate of grapes which one of her sons had walked miles to obtain for her stood on the table beside her bed; she pressed Laura to take some of these as she dared not eat them herself for fear they should make her milk disagree with the baby. Husband and sons had been unexpectedly helpful and sympathetic and she had been touched to the heart by their anxiety and their care for her; but for all that, she had felt relieved when she saw them depart for their work in the morning, leaving her with Mabel who, by virtue of her sex, could sympathise understandingly and give real practical aid.

When on that sunny, misty August morning at the beginning of the century, Laura said good-bye to Mrs Parkhurst and to all her other Heatherley friends and took the road over the heath to the railway station she thought the farewell was final. But Laura had not seen the last of her old landlady. Twenty years later, when she returned to live in the district,[41] one of her first callers was Mrs Parkhurst. A more cheerful, comfortable-looking and a much better-dressed Mrs Parkhurst than the one she remembered, but otherwise little changed. When Laura had formerly known her she had looked older than her years, but the time between then and their second meeting had adjusted that matter and at sixty-five she looked much as she had at forty-five.

She had brought with her an intelligent-looking, smartly-dressed girl of twenty whom she introduced as "My youngest daughter, Elsie; the one you saw last as a tiny long-clothed baby in bed. Do you see any change in her?" she asked, and her eyes dwelt proudly on the short-skirted, shingled, and pleasantly smiling figure at her side. Laura quite truthfully declared that had she not been told who she was she would never have recognised her, which caused some merriment and put all on a comfortable footing. They had come by bus, for buses were by that time running.[42] Mrs Parkhurst had somehow learned that Laura was again living in the district, and when Elsie had suggested taking her mother for a trip somewhere she at once thought of Laura, "for," she said, "I have never forgotten you. You ask Elsie here and she'll tell you how I've always talked about the way you used to run upstairs, two steps at a time very often, and what a one you were for your books and for bringing in great bunches of wild flowers." But it was not about Laura's youth she was longing to talk; that was over long ago and here she was, sitting at her own table with her own children around her, pouring out tea for her visitors, an accredited matron; but ready, as ever, to listen and be interested.

---

[41] Liphook, 1916–1928
[42] Buses started here in about 1920

Elsie—"my daughter Elsie"—was Mrs Parkhurst's chief topic of conversation. Elsie had been a wonderful child. "The flower of the family", her poor dad used to call her. He had been dead these five years, poor dear soul; he made a truly Christian end, so patient under suffering; and the boys were all married, and Mabel too, of course; she herself had been a grandmother for these seventeen years, and with the older children away from home, what she would have done without Elsie she did not know. Elsie was the clever one of the family. She had won a scholarship and been to a secondary school, and now she was book-keeper at one of the hotels, getting good money, and so good and thoughtful she wouldn't let her mother want for a thing. And she herself had not done too badly either; when the children had got up a little she had moved into a better house, one all to themselves, and had let the two front rooms to summer visitors, and since poor dad had been gone she had been drawing her little pension. "Thank God," she said, "I've got much to be thankful for."

The Jeromes[43]

"Bohemia" was a word on everybody's lips in those days. Like the old lady's Mesopotamia it was "a blessed word" which had a fine, sophisticated sound and could mean a great deal, or very little. An impromptu picnic, informal manners, an easy, careless style of dress, especially if it included big, loose bows, or bright colours, a friendship between two of opposite sexes, all passed as Bohemian with many who knew nothing of that country or its sea-coast. Others, and those of the kind not to be trifled with, classed as Bohemian those they suspected of loose morals, of not paying their debts, or of being incompetent housekeepers. It could be applied to a girl who had appeared in public with a little powder on her nose, to a woman who, having a maid, opened the front door herself to

---

[43] This chapter missing from previously published versions of *Heatherley*

visitors, or to a couple who were living together without marriage, or who starved their servants and beat their children. Any departure from convention, short of punishable crime was Bohemian.

There were at and around Heatherley several families of Bohemian repute, but with these Laura's contacts were but slight. Excepting in the matter of being privy to the contents of the telegrams they sent and received, some of those were certainly revealing, though not much more so than some others sent and received by strictly conventional families. In the days before the telephone was in general use, it was nothing out of the ordinary for an operator to handle a telegram of a hundred or more words in length and of the nature of a private letter. People in love with each other and therefore regardless of expense were in this way good customers of the Post Office Department.

Laura's introduction to Bohemia came about in this manner. She had for some time noticed with interest, and always on a Saturday, a rather peculiar looking couple at the post office counter. The husband was a large, tall man, past the prime of life, decidedly aristocratic looking, and with a voice and accent closely resembling that of elderly Victorian gentlemen in BBC broadcast plays. It was, as a matter of fact, the only instance in which Laura heard anything approaching that accent and intonation in real life. Perhaps she had been born too late, or it may be that they were not as general as is now supposed. Mr Jerome wore in summer a black alpaca jacket and a limp white Panama hat and often carried a large flag basket, such as workmen used at that time.

Mrs Jerome was a complete contrast to her husband. She was much younger, small, and what was then called 'dressy', and her English, though that of an educated woman, had a slight Cockney accent. She had been pretty in her youth and her features were still good, but, as such small, fair women so often do, she had worn badly. At forty, her complexion had faded, the skin of her neck had shrivelled, and the hair, which an artist had remarked when he painted it resembled sunshine, by that time was the colour of string. Yet she had the air of knowing herself to be an attractive woman, and she was an attractive woman. She had *chic*, wit and charm.

She was of French birth, though born and brought up in London, where her father had acted as official interpreter at a large railway terminus. And, all her life, she dressed the part of a Frenchwoman, favouring black for outdoor wear, with small, natty little hats, usually of her own concoction.

109

A loose quill in Mrs Jerome's hat—toque was the proper name for such hats when in fashion—introduced Laura to the couple. She asked for a pin, and, as it was a very quiet time, with no one but themselves in the office, and Laura had a needle and cotton handy, she offered to stitch it in for her. After that had been done, but not by Laura, for Mrs Jerome had seized the needle and had the quill set at the smartest possible angle in a trice, they remained chatting pleasantly for a few minutes, as people will do who feel themselves under some small obligation.

After that, they became more friendly at each visit, and, early in their acquaintanceship, Laura learned that Mrs Jerome was school-mistress in a neighbouring village. On Saturdays, the school holiday, they combined the pleasant walk between there and Heatherley with the transaction of their post office business, which, though it appeared ordinary to Laura, consisting mostly of buying stamps and posting letters, was, she was told, of too private a nature to be trusted to their own village postmistress. This seeming mystery was a mild one. Mr Jerome was a writer of short stories, and, until he became more successful than he had been up to that time, preferred that his ambition should not be known locally. Of course, as he remarked, there were the returned manuscripts, which "that demned, inquisitive old harridan" was bound to handle, but they might pass with her for wills, or bills, or the County Court summonses, as long as she did not see the addresses of those he sent away. It was a good thing that poor, innocent old Mrs Garbitt[44] could not hear what he said about her, which, however, was said with the highest good humour and all in the way of business—or what he called local colour, for Laura found afterwards that the inquisitive, gossiping old village postmistress was a stock figure in his stories of country life.

At their second or third visit after the quill incident, Laura was invited to tea with them on the next Sunday and soon she was told to come every Sunday, to come after the office closed in the morning and stay the whole day. During her last months at Heatherley she did spend some part of almost every Sunday there and would some-times walk over on weekday evenings after the office was closed, and she might have gone even more frequently, for she found their company most fascinating, had not Mr Jerome felt it necessary when dusk had fallen to escort her home to the very door. That was

---

[44] Possibly Mrs Gamblen, postmaster's wife in Headley at the time

due to his old-fashioned, punctilious code of manners. That a young lady should never be allowed out after dark without a male escort, that no lady of any age should open a room door for herself when a man or boy were in the room, that a man in saluting a lady should not merely raise his hat, but totally remove it in a sweeping bow, were canons either inherited, or so firmly engraved on his mind in his youth, that they were held sacred long after he had thrown off what he called the shackles of convention, including conventional religion and politics.

In religion he called himself an agnostic, in politics he tended to what would now be called the extreme Left. In literature alone he was a traditionalist, loving all that is best of past ages, yet, even in that, there was a twist that saddened Laura, for, although he knew what was best and could appreciate it, he aimed in his own writing at little above the lowest.

Reading aloud to the ladies while they did needlework was a special feature of family life as Mr Jerome had known it in his boyhood and when, after his long wanderings, he returned to home life, he was more than willing to revive the old custom. Some part of every Sunday when Laura was with them he read aloud. At first from such writers as Dickens, Thackeray and Thomas Hardy. He read well, though with some Victorian mannerisms, and he loved and admired the work of all the great writers, but even nearer to his heart was his own latest effort and when Laura had been tested and found worthy he would with many a modest ha and hum and clearing of the throat, read whatever he had written since she had last been there.

Then Laura was in a delicate position. She was proud to be trusted and liked to see him so happy and hopeful, but admire his writing she could not. It struck her and always struck her as a queer freak of human nature that one who knew and could appreciate all that was best in literature should fall to such a low level in his own writing. Not that that was unusual in real life, she often afterwards applied Meredith's lines "All the oceans tramp and roar to throw that faint white line upon the shore" to the best she herself could do after a lifetime spent in studying the best models; but at that time she had never before been on intimate terms with a writer, good, bad or indifferent, and she had an idea that according to a man's reading, so he would write.

Mr Jerome aimed, as he said, at writing a good magazine story, but his work was not favoured by magazine editors and only very occasionally by the editors of small penny weeklies.

Mr Jerome was fond of talking about plots. A plot, he said, must be worked out architecturally, and to aid him in this he had invented a system of graphs. Then every character must be true to type. He was very firm on that point. And local colour must be added to put flesh upon what he called the skeleton. The system sounded most impressive to Laura, and her disappointment was great when story after story he had written proved to be nothing more than a caricature of the most ordinary type of popular fiction. His hero and heroine had names, but needed them not, for they might just as well have been labelled hero and heroine; his guardian, for there was usually a guardian, who was so shifty in expression that the reader knew at once that he had appropriated the fortune of his ward, unless he happened to be the type of guardian who was destined to marry his ward, when he was younger, handsome and self-sacrificing. What he called his local colour consisted of the throwing in free, gratis and for nothing, of a few rustics speaking an unidentified dialect.

It was with mixed feelings that Laura heard from Mrs Jerome that her husband had put her in one of his stories. It was a great honour, of course, and a compliment, for she felt she could not be as uninteresting as she had thought if a story could be written about her, even one of Mr Jerome's stories. On the other hand, supposing it were published, and a few of his stories were published, what would people who knew her think when they read it. She need not have been afraid. When the story was read out by Mr Jerome, his eyes as often on her face as on his manuscript to ascertain the impression it made upon her, its heroine proved indeed to have the same colour eyes, hair and complexion as herself, but there the resemblance ended and she was soon free to enjoy the idea of herself in a white silk ball dress with a spray of pink roses on the shoulder. As she went to bed that night, feeling a little discontented because in real life she had never been to a ball or had an evening dress of any kind and was never likely to have one, she stood still suddenly while putting her nightdress over her head and said, "A fat lot he knows about me or any other girl!" Though poorly expressed, her saying was true. He knew no more than the outside appearance of her or anyone, perhaps not even excepting his wife, for one human being may adore another without the least understanding of their inner nature. A cynic might say that the less understanding the greater the adoration, and perhaps it is better for most people not to peer too closely into human nature and its motives, but a born writer has no need to peer, he sees by the light of his own nature.

Mr Jerome, then, was not a born writer, or, indeed a good, or a successful writer, but his writing had brought him into touch with writing men, chiefly journalists, and as often one or other of these ran down from town on a Sunday to see him, Laura had the advantage of hearing their conversation. By that time she had been promoted to pouring out at the tea table, Alicia preferring to lie back in her easy chair with her teacup balanced upon the arm, while she puffed at her cigarette with a detached, yet faintly amused expression. The men would sit at the table for an hour, talking shop, as they called it, and Laura would not have missed a word of this talk for worlds. It is not to be supposed that Gustavious Salisbury, Mr Pennington-White or any of the others with equally impressive names were at then top of their profession, but to Laura at that time they were accepted as being so, and when 'the Street' or the office of such-and-such a periodical were mentioned casually, she was puffed up with pride at the thought that at last she was moving in literary circles. Sometimes one of them would take away with him one of Mr Jerome's short stories which all present had agreed needed only a personal introduction to immediately be accepted by an editor, and although this happened time after time with no result, a few weeks of hopeful expectation followed. Mrs Jerome once told Laura that at such times Mr Jerome would stand inside the front door watching the letter box for half an hour before the postman could possibly arrive, his nerves on edge and his attitude tense with anxiety, which manifestation she attributed to his artistic temperament. The usual outcome was that, after weeks of suspense, the manuscript was returned by the friend who had volunteered to negotiate, or the friend might forget to return and, when a pressing invitation to come down for a Sunday put him in mind of it, he would bring it back in his pocket. Laura often wondered if Alicia had the great faith she professed in her husband's future as a writer.

There was no official schoolhouse and their home was one of a row of small detached modern cottages. Laura afterwards declared that on her first visit she would have known the house to be theirs by its outside appearance. All the other houses in the row had stiff white lace curtains, tied back, but not too far back lest the neighbours look in, with broad ribbon sashes while the windows at

Number Nine had plain dark green curtains, pulled well back. The Jeromes used the best, front downstairs room as a living room and took their meals there, often at summer suppertime with the curtains undrawn after the lamp was lighted, liking, as they said, to see the night sky and breath the fresh air. This habit of theirs, together with others, such as Mrs Jerome's occasional cigarette, and their way of walking out into the fields together with no hats on, rather scandalised their near neighbours. But they were very well liked in the village, for Mrs Jerome was well esteemed as a teacher who had her pupils well in hand, and, as to Mr Jerome, anybody could see that he was a gentleman born. Though how they came to get married at their time of life, and her with a good salary and home of her own, puzzled most of the villagers. Some were inclined to think that Mr Jerome had married for a home and was living on his wife's earnings, but, against that, she spent money more freely in the matter of charring and laundry than formerly. Surely, they said, if she'd just taken him in as a kindness, he'd have done the housework himself while she was at school, instead of just doing the garden and all that letter-writing. There he sat, at that writing-desk right slap in front of the window, hour after hour, writing away for dear life, anybody might go and look right in the window and he wouldn't know or take any notice. Peculiar, that was what they were, a bit peculiar, which being translated became Bohemian.

Their living room delighted Laura, for as well as what she thought fine paintings on the walls, there were various curios Mr Jerome had collected on his travels and books everywhere. A well-filled bookcase reached to the ceiling and an overflow of books on tables and chairs, and even on the floor in one corner. These last she was told were waiting for new shelves to be fixed in a recess by the fireplace, but they were still piled in the corner nine months later, when Laura left Heatherley. The other rooms were similarly crowded with the contents of the packing cases Mr Jerome had brought to an already well-filled house. But the Jeromes lived cheerfully in spite of the disorder, and very comfortably. Laura opened her eyes widely on one chilly summer evening when one of them proposed a fire should be lighted and the other put a match to the one already laid in the grate. When, thinking it had been lighted at least partly for her own comfort, she remarked that it seemed a pity to soil the grate, Alicia, for she was Alicia to Laura by that time, laughed and said carelessly, "Mrs Brown will have to clear the mess up. She doesn't come tomorrow for it is her washing day, but she'll be here on Tuesday morning, and we can stand the emu feather screen in front of the grate to hide the ashes." Another habit which in Laura's eyes marked Alicia as Bohemian was sewing on Sunday. She had always something of her own to repair or bring up to date. When ruching had gone out and tucks were in fashion she would spend a whole Sunday unpicking and pressing and stitching the front of one of her blouses. Then she had her almost weekly millinery bout. Her talent in this line almost amounted to magic. She would take a few square inches of velvet, ruffle, stitch, pat and pull it, stick a quill at one side, or drape it with a veil, then, holding it at arms length, say, "How do you like my new toque?" "Three guineas at Heath's," her husband would say promptly, and, at least to Laura's unsophisticated eyes it did look much the same as those small, expensive hats from the best shops which were known as creations. Her husband took great pride in his wife's dress. "Trust a Frenchwoman's taste!" he would say to Laura; but what Laura thought the most endearing feature in them both was the great zest and enjoyment they extracted from everything.

It was an exciting experience to her to sit at a tea-table where the master of the house drank unsweetened tea from a glass, with a slice of lemon floating on the surface and, after tea, the lady of the house smoked cigarettes, and, more exciting still to listen to their talk at table. Mrs Jerome so vivacious and witty, with a keen edge to her wit which amounted at times to malice, and her husband, more humorous than witty, telling some story of his youth in London, or of some adventure he had had on his travels. He belonged to a family of artists. His brother, he said, had been praised as a colourist by Ruskin, and only his early death had prevented his rising to fame. Though not a painter himself, Mr Jerome had known Burne-Jones, Watts and Rossetti, and others whose names were by that time well known in art and literature. He said he had himself been the bad boy of the family and, excepting for a few years as a medical student, had settled to no profession. While still a very young man he had joined in the rush for the Australian gold fields, raising no gold, but, as he expressed it, digging hard for experience. After that, he had become a prospector for metals in South Africa, a tea planter in India, finally, he had turned trader and in that way made enough of a fortune to enable him to return and live in a modest way in his native country.

Then he and his wife were deeply in love with each other. Laura had had no idea before that middle-aged people could be in love, but these were, she was sure of that, not only because they made no secret of it, but by the way they looked at and spoke to each other. At first she was a little shocked that it should be so, for it was contrary to all she had learned from the novelists. Love, according to them, was the prerogative of the young and fair, or at least the interesting-looking, excepting of course Esmond and his Lady Castlewood, but when she heard the Jerome's love story, she found it as exciting as any novel.

One day, when she had known her for some time, Alicia took off a thin gold ring, set with a garnet, which she wore above her wedding ring and pointed to her own name engraved inside it, "Alicia." That, she said, was my engagement ring, but it was not a new one, when the name was engraved, I was just a month old. Then she told Laura that, on the day she was born, her mother was taken ill prematurely. She was out at the time, but managed to get home unaided and say to their one small servant: "Call somebody," and the maid, in a great fright, rushed to the door and begged a lady who happened to be passing if she would come to her mistress. The lady, although a stranger, came in, got the patient to bed and summoned doctor and nurse and remained in the house until Alicia was born. After that, the elder Mrs Jerome and Alicia's mother became close friends.

That lady was Mr Jerome's mother, he being then a youth of eighteen. Naturally, when the time for christening the baby came, she was asked to be little Alicia's godmother, and, on that occasion, Alicia's father, in what his daughter when telling the story called "his graceful French way," presented the ring engraved with the baby's name, Alicia, as a small token of his gratitude.

From that time a close friendship existed between the two families. The Jeromes were much better-off and lived in a larger and more comfortable house than the Denairs, and the elder Jeromes were much older than Alicia's parents, but otherwise they had much in common, both couples being lively happy-go-lucky people with little regard for convention, surrounded in their respective streets with neighbours of the heavily respectable Victorian type. By the time little Alicia could toddle she felt herself as much at home in her 'Auntie' Jerome's house as she did in that of her parents. The Jerome's house had a garden, the Denair's had none, and when Mrs Jerome knew that her friend was especially busy, or when it was a finer day than usual, Alicia would be fetched by herself or one of her boys to play on the lawn beneath the apple tree there. Wilmot, who did much of his studying at home, was the one usually sent to fetch her. He often went on his own initiative, for he was remarkably fond of the little girl, so much so, that his devotion to her became a family joke in both families. He would lie at full length on his back on the grass and hold her above him at arm's length, carry her pick-a-back round the garden, or play at bears or lions with her among the gooseberry bushes. He said himself in after years that when he once had been left in charge of her and she appeared to be uncomfortable he had changed her napkin. That may have been said to tease his wife, but it was at least certain that he as a nearly grown-up young man had shown an extraordinary interest in and love of little Alicia. And, family tradition added, she had been so fond of her Motand, as she called him, that often when he had taken her home and turned to go she had stretched out her arms and cried.

She had been too young at that time to remember all that, for, before she was two years old, Wilmot Jerome had abandoned his medical studies and left home, without permission being asked or granted, to join in the rush for the Australian gold fields. According to his own account, he raised no gold, though his hard labour brought him a rich haul of experiences. He was next heard of by his family prospecting for metals in South Africa, then as tutor to the sons of a diamond merchant on the Rand, and, finally, as a trader at Beira. The Denair family heard nothing further of his adventurous life, for, by that time, both Mr and Mrs Jerome had died and their only son living in England had married and gone from the district.

By the time she had reached the age of thirty, Alicia was also an orphan. She had taken up teaching and, after her time at a Training College, had left London for Yorkshire where she remained for many years. She loved the North of England people for their sincerity and outrightness of speech. "No humbug about *them*," she would say when speaking about them, but, strangely for one so communicative in general, that was almost all Laura ever heard her say about her long sojourn among them. Excepting that she had three times been engaged to be married and once come very near to the day of the intended ceremony, but she had, as she expressed it, always thought better of it before the actual knot was tied. So there were long blank, or semi-blank spaces in the life story of both husband and wife as known to Laura.

Three years before Laura knew her she had come south, to escape, she said, from her last marriage engagement, and taken up her then present post in a Hampshire village. She had settled down, as she thought, to perpetual spinsterhood, busy and happy in her work, with her hobby of dress to amuse her spare hours, and her pension to look forward to, her only regret being caused by the total absence of anyone with her own tastes or temperament with whom to associate, when Wilmot Jerome re-appeared.

He had returned to England, hoping to spend the rest of his life there, not with a fortune, far from it, but with sufficient means to maintain an old bachelor in modest comfort and, finding she was the only survivor of those he had left light-heartedly and without a farewell as a young man, he had determined to track down Alicia. He managed, after some trouble, to do this, and came down to Hampshire to see her, thinking only to stay a day or two and talk over old times, but he stayed on, week after week, at the small inn where he had put up, supposedly for the fishing, and, before the summer ended they had been secretly married one Saturday morning in the nearest large town. Their marriage was a secret one and was, for some time kept secret, because at that time, under the authorities she was subject to, a woman teacher was expected to resign her appointment upon marriage. She had no wish to give up her work or the prospect of the pension due to her in a few years.

Although her husband had sufficient means to keep them both comfortably in a small way, after her independent life, she said, she would hate to be dependant upon another, especially upon the man she loved so passionately. Love should be a gift, she told Laura, not a matter of work and wages. And when Laura, who knew quite well that that marriage meant more than that, said, "Marriage is often work without wages," she said that was worse still. The secret of their marriage was soon out, however, a man whether a stranger or locally-known cannot be seen visiting the home of a village school-mistress at all hours without causing scandal. The clergyman, who was one of the school managers, interviewed Alicia and had to be told of the marriage. He, personally, was against the compulsory retirement of married school teachers and promised to use his influence with the county authorities to make an exception in her case. Meanwhile Alicia continued her teaching and her husband came to live at her house, and no decision as to her retirement was reached during the time Laura knew the Jeromes.

'I have had playmates, I have had companions…'

One winter afternoon when the oil-lamp which swung over the post-office counter had been lighted at half-past three and all who had no urgent business to compel them to face the east wind were enjoying their tea and muffins by the fireside, the office door suddenly burst open to admit a young man. He was a stranger to Laura, but nevertheless welcome, as anyone else would have been who brought a little variety into a dull day. He was a large young man, both tall and thickset, and the shaggy grey overcoat he was wearing made him look larger than he would otherwise have done. A snub nose and remarkably clear bright grey eyes were the only noticeable features of a face whipped into rosiness by the wind and rain. His small fair moustache and the shaggy grey surface of his overcoat were beaded with raindrops and he carried a stout walking-stick of some natural wood. A farmer, or a game-keeper, thought Laura.

Her guess was wide of the mark. Richard Brownlow,[45] though not a Londoner by birth, had spent almost the whole of his life in London, the last few years employed by one of the big cable companies in the City. He had come to Heatherley to stay with some connections by marriage who had recently settled there. He was evidently a cheerful and communicative young man. As he handed in his telegram he remarked that he knew his mother would not rest until she had heard of his safe arrival, and added that he had walked the last ten miles of the way and had enjoyed the wild weather. "This east wind which shrivels most people up is the breath of life to me," he declared.

When Laura returned to the counter after sending off his telegram he was still there, examining a showcase of picture postcards with local views. Alma being away for an hour, Laura should have summoned Mrs Hertford to attend to him as a shop customer, but having nothing to do herself at the moment and perhaps wishing to see more of him, she helped him to select and took the money for his purchases. The discussion of picture-postcard views led to the discussion of the scenes represented, and it was not until another customer claimed her attention that he made his exit.

Alma had by that time returned to duty, and when Laura said that she did not think she had seen that young man before, she answered thickly—she was sucking a sweet at the time—"You'll see him again." Which was odd, because, as Alma afterwards said, she herself had never seen him before and did not know him from Adam. She had concluded from his appearance that he was on a walking tour. The term 'hiking' was unknown in those days.

Laura did see Richard Brownlow again. During his first short visit to Heatherley he called at the post office several times daily, and after that he was frequently down for weekends and longer holidays. The friendship which was soon established between them grew rapidly, for it was founded on mutual liking and similarity of taste. Everything in literature Laura admired, Richard admired. If one of the two began to quote poetry, the other capped the quotation, or held out a finger to link and called out the name of a poet to signify that their thoughts had been identical. And often the old childish proceeding did not end there, for the poet's name which first sprung to the lips of one would spring to the lips of the other.

---

[45] See Notes at end of book for a possible identity of Richard Brownlow

"Burns!" "Browning!" or "Keats!" they would cry simultaneously, and instead of linked fingers there were clasped hands and laughter.

Richard had an only sister named Mavis who sometimes came with him to Heatherley. The two were devoted and their tastes were alike. Both were fond of ideas, especially ideas for reforming the world; both loved the country and both were well read. In appearance the two were very unlike, Richard being large, and Mavis a slender graceful little creature with dark red hair, eyes the colour of autumn beech leaves and a velvety cream complexion. She was so small and dainty of build and so quick and bird-like in her movements that, beside her, Laura, herself neither large nor inactive, felt clumsy. She had mental qualities to match her physique; she did not reason things out to a logical conclusion as Richard did, but reached her conclusions by flashes of insight or by wheeling and dipping in a kind of swallow flight which, light and casual as it might appear, was certain. Laura was delighted with her new friends. She would have liked them in any case for what they were in themselves, but an added attraction for her was that they were modern. They had the latest ideas, knew and sometimes used the latest catchwords, and had read and could discuss new books by new authors whose names, to Laura, were but vaguely familiar. At last, Laura thought, she had friends who were truly *fin de siècle*.

On dark nights, after the post office had closed, they would take long walks, swinging along the highway, Mavis on Richard's arm on one side, Laura on the other, chanting in unison the quatrains of Omar Khayyám, or a chorus from Swinburne, or talking sense or nonsense. Often they were in melancholy mood, as they imagined became children of a decadent day, and a silent passer-by who had happened to overhear their outpourings might have pitied them. How many times did Laura exclaim tragically into the night:

> What shall I be at fifty, if God should keep me alive,
> Who find my life so bitter before I am twenty-five?

or "thank whatever powers there be" that

> No man lives for ever,
> That dead men rise up never,

in pure innocent ignorance of bitterness of spirit, or the terrible finality of death. May the sins of youth be forgiven! Mavis, equally inexperienced, would cry aloud in tragic tones such lines as,

Would to God I had never known you, sweet,
Would to God we had never met,
To steer a way for our erring feet
To the sad shores of regret!

while Richard, tall as a cliff and firm as a rock between them, preserved the mental as well as the physical balance by keeping mainly
to passages from Milton or Shakespeare.

One night when they had climbed to the summit of a hill where
a tall granite cross marked the spot where had once stood a gibbet,[46]
Laura dropped to her knees on the turf and, pressing her ear to the
cold stone of the shaft, recited in trance-like tones an imaginary
conversation between two malefactors who she asked them to
suppose had once suffered there, an effort which was applauded as
worthy of Poe.

On Sunday afternoons and light summer evenings Laura
showed Richard and Mavis some of her moorland and woodland
haunts. Some, not all; there were a few spots she reserved. One of
these was the place she had named 'the heart of the wood', where an
oblong of lawn-like turf, threaded by a little stream, was shut in on
every side by trees and thick undergrowth. Ferns grew beside the
stream and on one side a spreading beech tree cast in summer a cool
green shade. Laura had often gone there on summer evenings, to
think her own quiet thoughts, to read—although when she took a
book there she seldom opened it—or simply to steep herself in the
beauty and peace of her surroundings. There had been a time when
she had hurried there with hot, angry tears in her eyes, caused by the
slighting remark of a chance-met acquaintance. The remark was
probably unconsidered and in no way intended as an insult, but it is
mortifying to youthful pride to be reminded that one has neither the
birth, education, nor any personal quality to justify the holding of an
opinion differing from those held by the majority. But there, in the
wood, was healing for sore eyes and hurt pride. 'Woodsorrel and
wild violet' to 'soothe the heart's fret', and what drooping spirits
can long remain sullen within hearing of a blackbird's evensong?

But although Laura held inviolate this and one or two other
secret sanctuaries, she admitted her new friends to all her ordinary
haunts. She showed them the view from the pine-clump, Bob's
valley farm, and many woodland nooks other than her own special
retreat. They loved the country and never tired of exploring its

---

[46] Gibbet Hill, Hindhead

beauties, though, as she soon found, their love of nature, though perhaps equal in degree, was of a different kind from her own. To her the country was an enveloping atmosphere from which she drew strength and delight; they studied it consciously, as an open book, naming each bird and flower, or never resting until they could name them, surveying prospects in detail to discover what in its contours gave charm to the view; examining the ferns, lichens, and wild-flowers and looking them up in their little books which gave the names of the species in Latin. Their interest was intelligent, Laura's instinctive.

She showed them one day, far out on the moors, a patch of heather which, seen from a short distance, looked stunted and blighted and had a reddish tinge. When closely examined every individual plant was seen to be netted and dragged down to earth by the thin, red, threadlike runners of a parasite. They were horrified at the sight and asked the name of the plant with the stranglehold. Laura told them it was dodder and said that, if she were a novelist, she would write a book with that title. It would be the story of a man or woman—she thought a woman—of fine, sensitive nature, bound by some tie—probably marriage—to one of a nature which was strong, coarse, and encroaching, and would tell how, in time, the heather person shrank and withered, while the dodder one fattened and prospered.

It was not a cheerful idea, but it pleased them, and they sat for some time on a grassy knoll overlooking the heather patch, eating from a bag of cherries Richard had produced and discussing Laura's plot. Then one of them spoke of the dodder husband as the villain of the piece. "No!" cried Laura, quite warmly, rushing to the defence of her newly-born character. "The dodder cannot help being dodder, it was made that way, and must act according to its nature, and in the same way, the dodder man has no evil intentions, he may even be kindly disposed; it just happens that his close proximity is ruinous. He thrives and becomes more and more bumptious, important, and respected—I think he must be a stockbroker, with a white waistcoat and a thick gold watch-chain—she—she painted quite good watercolours when a girl you know—she withers and shrinks into the mere wraith of a woman."

"Jolly fine!" said Richard. "But who is going to write this story?" "Laura, of course," said Mavis, "she knows all about people." At that, Richard looked a little taken aback, for he, as the man of the party and a man with known literary tastes, was obviously best fitted to deal with the delicate situation. But though touched with the sense of masculine superiority (for how could he help it, being a child of his own day?), he was touched but slightly. He sprang to his feet, seized Laura's hand, and having heaved her up, waltzed her round and round on a patch of sand, singing, "She knows about it all. She knows! She knows!"

Their more serious talk was in essence not unlike that of young people of their type today. They had theories about many things of which by experience they knew nothing, and their theories did credit to their hearts, if not always to their heads. They hated the oppressor and pitied the oppressed. The miseries of the women chain-makers of Cradley Heath, then much in the limelight, or those of the sweated seamstresses of the East End of London, moved Richard to wrath. The mention of the shoeless, ragged, half-starved children of the slums touched Mavis and Laura to tears. They called it a burning shame that human beings should be compelled to live in houses no better than cattle byres, and that workers should be underpaid, ill-fed, or suffer any kind of injustice. So far they resembled the young of today in their ideas, but only so far, for although they were aware of and deplored social ills, they had no plan for their redress. The mild Liberalism in which they believed would in time, they hoped, ameliorate the lot of the poor and oppressed; but when and to what extent they had no idea. With old Omar they longed to grasp this sorry scheme of things entire and shatter it to bits, but they possessed no blueprint by which to remould it nearer to their hearts' desire. Had they been born half a century later, how they would have enjoyed helping to plan the New Order!

But though, as is the way of youth, they were inclined to take themselves seriously, there were times when they talked sheer non-sense. They were fond of limericks and other nonsense verses, and between them had a good stock of these. Richard knew several of the *Bab Ballads* by heart and could, and would, fill up a blank space in the conversation by declaiming *The Rival Curates* or *The Precocious Baby,* often with Mavis trying to stuff her handkerchief into his mouth to stop him. When other entertainment failed they would relate anecdotes. Laura had her country childhood to draw upon for her stories and her 'Lawk 'a' mussy O's and 'Where be 'ee a-gooin's provoked peals of laughter. Richard's and Mavis's stories were more sophisticated, with a sting in the tail. Brilliantly clever, thought Laura.

The truth of the matter is, though no-one would have attributed it to such a cause at that date, that those bubbling high spirits, that love of childish nonsense, that reeling with laughter without cause, were due to a rebound; in Laura's case from a somewhat harsh and restricted childhood, and in that of her friends, from experiencing a great shock, followed by a prolonged ordeal. Laura had not known Richard and Mavis long before she surmised from chance words that there was, or had been, some shadow upon their home life, and when the time was ripe for confidences, Mavis, who had come to her room one night, told her the whole story. Laura had said that her people were poor, and when Mavis retorted, "Well, all the best people are poor, aren't they?" she had answered, "But not poor in the way I mean. We live in a tiny cottage and my father is a working man." Mavis said in a subdued voice, "But how lucky you are to have a father." Then she had told her the main points of the following story.

Richard and Mavis had been well educated and had had a happy, comfortable home with kind parents in childhood and early youth. Then, five years before Laura knew them, their father had died suddenly in bed by the side of their mother, who had known nothing of his collapse until she woke up naturally and touching his hand found it cold. The shock had shattered her nervous system and left her more or less an invalid. For a year after her husband's death her reason had been feared for and she had been taken from hospital to hospital and from nursing home to nursing home in the hope of a cure. The only near relative of the family then living was a sister of Mrs Brownlow who lived far up in the North of England and whose husband was then in delicate health. After she had done all she could to help the young Brownlows to settle their affairs she had been obliged to return to her own home, and the two, Richard at that time not quite twenty and Mavis eighteen, had been left alone to face hitherto undreamed-of responsibilities.

At their father's death the greater part of the family income had ceased, but they were not left utterly destitute. Richard was already earning a small salary. Their father had insured his life for a fairly substantial sum, and his late employers, a City firm, generously paid his widow a sum equal to a full year of his earnings. The greater part of this small capital went in specialists' and nursing-home fees, but it also sufficed to keep the home going until Richard was earning enough, though barely enough, for them to live upon. Since then he had had annual increases, although his salary, according to their standards, was still but a modest one. At the time of her father's death Mavis had begun a course of art training with the idea of taking up the new poster and advertisement work. She had a gift for drawing and her teachers had a good opinion of her as a colourist; but her training then came to a premature end and she had to turn housekeeper. It may be supposed that a girl of eighteen, without any previous experience beyond that of the light, ornamental duties of an indulged only daughter in the school holidays, found housekeeping difficult and housework drudgery. Richard, at twenty, had not only to undertake the full financial responsibility of the home, but also that of his mother's illness. Mavis told Laura that he would sometimes sit at the table the whole evening, half the time adding up totals and pencilling columns of figures, and the other half with his elbows on the table and his head in his hands.

It must have been a hard life for two young things who had hitherto been spared all responsibility by loving and protecting parents; but when their mother had recovered sufficiently to return home their position became even harder, for Mrs Brownlow's recovery was but partial. The kind mother they had formerly known had become a capricious, fractious, self-centred semi-invalid, what we should now call a nervous wreck, and although they knew that this sad change in her was due to the shock she had experienced, and never failed her in their love and sympathy, they must have suffered severely. To her duties as housekeeper Mavis had added those of nurse. The management of their slender resources still devolved upon Richard.

For more than a year their lives were overshadowed. Then gradually Mrs Brownlow's condition improved. She became able to dress herself without help, to do a little in the house, to go for a walk in the park, or to look at the shops, and although she was still at times irritable and capricious she was not more so than the ordinary nerve sufferer. Small pleasures again brightened the lives of her children, they could go to a lecture, or to the theatre, or on Sunday take train for some wayside station in Surrey and tramp back over the hills. Both had always been great readers and, even in the thick of their troubles, reading and discussing the books they read had been one unfailing resource. Now they found friends of their own age who shared their interest. They had gained experience, too, and felt more sure of themselves; they had accepted their position and learned to get the best out of it. In short, they had grown up.

A few weeks before Richard's first visit to Heatherley Mrs Brownlow's sister, recently widowed, had come to live with them and it was arranged that she should relieve Mavis of the housekeeping, leaving her free to learn shorthand and typing with a view to a post in the City. Mavis would have preferred to resume her art training, but that would have been longer, more expensive, and less certain as a means of livelihood. Their Aunt Maggie, they both declared, was an angel. As soon as she had taken the household reins in hand everything seemed to go smoothly, and as the elder sister she had great influence on their mother who, under her care, became more like her old self. As soon as she had taken stock of the situation, Aunt Maggie suggested that Richard and Mavis should have some little change of air and scene occasionally. Neither had slept from home for one night since the last family holiday in the Isle of Wight the year of their father's death. Aunt Maggie said that such a closed-in life at their age was unnatural. A nephew of her late husband had recently gone to live at Heatherley, there was lovely country round there, and his wife took in paying guests. Why should not Richard go there for his next long weekend? Richard went.

Both Richard and Mavis were anxious that Laura should get work in London. They sketched a delightful programme of theatres, museums, and picture galleries and of country outings on Sundays, with themselves as companions, and for a time Laura was persuaded that the change would be wholly delightful. She even went so far as to obtain a syllabus of some Civil Service examination, to pay her fee of one guinea to a Civil Service college, and to begin studying the subjects. But she knew from the first she could not hope to win even the lowest place in a competitive examination no matter how hard she studied. Her education had left too many black spaces and, apart from that, she had not a competitive mind. The correspondence course only served to reveal to herself her abysmal ignorance. Having never learned the rules, she had to leave most of the arithmetic problems unsolved. Her geography was a little better because she had read a good deal about foreign countries; but even so, she had not read the right books to enlighten her about imports and exports, or industries or distances. In essaywriting she was able to reach the average number of marks, sometimes a little above the average, though her paper often came back to her marked in red ink, 'More facts, please', or 'No purple patches'. Her handwriting alone was pronounced 'satisfactory'.

Her inborn peasant thrift, however, forbade wasting the guinea paid in advance and she persevered in at least conscientiously attempting to answer the questions and work out the problems. The guinea, which seemed quite a large sum to her, was of course very little as a fee for what the advertisement of the college termed 'individual tuition', and the comments of her coach were naturally brief and not very enlightening. But there was on one occasion a human touch. Then the subject set for the essay was: 'Give an account of a book you have read recently', and Laura, who at that time was enthralled by the work of Henry James, took for her subject *The Portrait of a Lady*. When her papers were returned to her, below the official red-ink assessment she found written, 'A curious choice. Don't care for James's work myself, but almost thou persuadest me!'

When Alma had mastered the telegraph instrument and could be left in charge for the two hours on Sunday morning, Laura had the exciting adventure of a trip to town. Richard and Mavis met her at Waterloo, and each of them seizing an arm, dragged her through the, to her, immense and confusing crowd on the platform. They appeared to be as much at home in the press as she was far out on the heath, but she, as they passed out of the station into the crowded gas-lit streets, had a dreamlike feeling of unreality.

It had been raining; the inside of their bus was choked to the doorway, and Richard assisted the two girls up the steep steps to the outside seats on the top of the vehicle. "Now we can talk", he said, as he turned back the tarpaulin which protected unoccupied seats from the rain, and they did try to talk, but the others soon saw that, with the roar of the traffic in her unaccustomed ears, Laura could not hear one half of what they were saying. So, huddled together for warmth, they sat in silence, smiling into each other's eyes when they happened to meet, while the horse-bus went, clopping and grinding, with many stops and much pinging of the bell, through lighted streets thronged with people, though the hour seemed quite late to Laura.

It was the first time she had seen London or any large town by night and, after her dark walk to the railway station and her hour in the dimly lit carriage, the scene she beheld from between the rails at the top of the bus was at first dazzling. But she soon found herself gazing down with deep interest on the flaring shop-fronts and the crowds surging before them, looking like crowds of little black ants against the brightness. In the roadway passed other buses with brightly lit interiors where the large, feathered hats of the women eclipsed the bowlered heads of the men, and the driver, sitting aloft and aloof on his high perch in front in his shining black macintosh cape, cracked his long whip and craned his neck to shout in a voice like a fog-horn to some passing fellow-driver. And there were hansoms jink-jinking as they threaded the heavier traffic and out-stripped it, and a one-legged man playing an accordion outside a public house, and children playing in the gutter, actually playing, with so much traffic about, and at that hour! And the smell and taste of the thick, moist air! What was it? It appeared to be a blend of orange-peel, horse-manure and wet clothes, with a dash of coal gas.

So this was London at night. And this noisy, hustling life beneath the street lamps was going on only a few miles away from the dark, silent, deserted heaths, fields, and woods she had left so recently. She had of course known that London was thickly popu-lated, that it was brightly lit at night, and that night crowds congre-gated, but it was not until she saw it with her own eyes that she fully realised the contrast between town and country. She fancied herself caught in a great sparkling net hanging amidst miles and miles of surrounding darkness.

"We shall soon be there. Only one other very short ride after this," said a voice in her ear, and she found that Richard had changed seats with Mavis and was sitting beside her. "Cold?" he asked, pressing her hand. "What do you think of London?" asked Mavis, and when Laura said that she thought it was wonderful they laughed and called her their little country mouse.

Richard and Mavis lived with their mother and aunt in a flat, or rather the upper floor of a house, in a pleasant suburban road. In the small plot in front of the house the leaves of wet evergreen shrubs reflected the light from a nearby lamp-post. The sound of the traffic in the main streets was subdued by distance to a dull roaring, against which their own footfalls and those of the few passers-by rang out sharply. Laura compared herself to some storm-buffeted ship which had reached a quiet harbour.

Richard and Mavis thought and sometimes spoke of themselves as poor, and Laura knew they must be much poorer than they had been in their father's lifetime, but their poverty was different in kind, as well as in degree, from that to which she had been accus-tomed. Some of the furniture in their rooms was shabby, because, as they explained, nothing had been renewed and very little renovated for more than five years, but it was good and substantial and tastefully disposed; the rooms had a look of inevitable rightness. They had treasures, too, which had belonged to former generations of their family. Oil-painted portraits of their grandparents hung on either side of the fireplace; blue and white china and a carved ivory pagoda brought home from abroad by a seafaring great-uncle were displayed in a cabinet, and a musical album, purchased by a great-aunt at the Great Exhibition, was brought out from a cupboard to play its little tinkling fairy-like tunes for Laura's amusement. Between its pages were tinted photographs of chignoned and crino-lined ladies, their gold chains and bracelets picked out with gilding; untinted photographs of whiskered men in dark cut-away coats and pale, wide trousers, their top-hats and gloves reposing beside them on elaborate studio tables.

This background reminded Laura of her father's family, but it was far removed from that of her own cottage home, and when she went to bed in Mavis's room, Mavis sleeping with her aunt that night, and found a fire burning and a hot water bottle in her bed, her surroundings seemed positively luxurious. By that time it was Sunday morning, for after the mother and aunt had retired the three friends had sat talking and Richard had read aloud stories and poems which fairly scintillated with brilliance, from some back numbers of *The Yellow Book* he had picked up on a second-hand bookstall.

To be actually in London for a night and a day in the company of her brilliant friends was exciting to Laura, and to be cared for and made much of, as they cared for and made much of her, was comforting to one who lived far from her own home and was dependent on herself alone for her well-being. The aunt, as they had said, was a perfect angel. She took care of them all and obviously enjoyed seeing their enjoyment, so that Laura would have had a weekend of unalloyed bliss, had it not been for the disquieting presence of Mrs Brownlow. Her affliction had by that time taken the form of a constant twitching of the features and a restlessness, which would not allow her to sit down in one chair for more than a moment or two. She would come into the room where her children and Laura were talking, wander from chair to chair, complain that the fire was too large, or too low, then drift out again. If anyone spoke at all loudly she would remind them of her 'poor head'; if she required anything and no one had noticed her requirement, she complained that no one ever did anything for her.

Her manner towards Laura was polite, though by no means cordial, except on one occasion when Laura was relating some trifling experience which the others found amusing and she, with a shrug of impatience, audibly muttered "What nonsense!" Richard, who had been present and seen Laura's embarrassment, said to her afterwards, "You mustn't take any notice of Mother's little ways. She's been ill so long, I'm afraid we have spoiled her", and Mavis sighed and said "If only Laura could have known her as she used to be when we were children! She'd have loved her then."

Early in the afternoon Richard suggested that he and Mavis should show Laura the City before seeing her off at Waterloo, and after some bus rides and tea at a tea-shop they walked through silent Sabbath streets, the names of which were familiar to Laura through her telegraph work, but which, until then, had been but names. Now she saw Fleet Street and Johnson's Court, passing without the faintest anticipatory thrill the office of the magazine whose editor would one day accept her first shyly-offered contribution; then on to Threadneedle Street to gaze on the outside of the Central Telegraph Office, familiarly known to Laura as 'T.S.' and figuring in her world as the centre of the universe. Now and then a horse-bus trundled through the main streets and a few passengers were seen on the pavement; the side streets were deserted. And, strange as it seemed to Laura, although Richard and Mavis had lived all their lives in London, neither of them had ever before seen the City on a Sunday afternoon. They had known it only as the thronged hive of weekdays, and the hushed calm which seemed positively to brood over the empty ways appeared to amaze them almost as much as it did Laura. They wandered on, walking leisurely and stopping to look at this and that in places past which on an ordinary day they would have been carried by a swift tide of humanity. They passed through between high blocks of buildings narrow passages where their footsteps rang loudly on the pavement and the sky, tinged with sunset, showed like a rose-coloured ribbon between the tall roofs.

That walk through the silent, deserted City was one of the richest memories of Laura's later years. She would not for anything have missed seeing it as it was then; nor would she have willingly missed seeing the very different Saturday night scene in the shopping quarter, or the suburban home of her friends; and still less would she have cared to miss the sensation of freedom and home-coming she felt when, at the end of her train journey, she came to the heath and once more breathed the odours of heather and pine and saw the starry heaven above the pine-tops.

It had been delightful to visit her friends in London and to obtain a brief glimpse of town life. She would like to go often. If ever she became rich she would have a flat of her own to go to for a few days whenever she felt inclined. But never to make her home there, shut away by miles and miles of bricks and mortar from the green earth and the changing seasons. To see the first swallow skim the fields and streams, to hear the first cuckoo call from the woods, to see the apple trees in blossom and the other flowers as they appeared, from the earliest snowdrop through all the pageant of spring and summer to the golden-green ivy bloom, alive with bees and hovering butterflies, was, she- felt instinctively, essential to her bodily and spiritual well-being.

When she had left London the weather, though no longer wet, had been moist and mild. The Hampshire night was clear and frosty and when she reached the higher ground she found a light sprinkling of snow. She breathed in the pure, invigorating air with conscious enjoyment and rejoiced in her sense of release from the flaring lights and eddying crowd to the freedom of her natural environment.

The next day she wrote to the secretary of her Civil Service college saying that, since she had little chance of gaining a place in the examinations and had a fairly good post where she was, she had decided to discontinue her course at the end of that session. And so ended Laura's one bid for worldly advancement. Her compensation for failure in that respect was a whole lifetime spent, if not all of it actually in the country, never too far from it to be able to reach it easily. During many years of her later life she had both sea and country just beyond her doorstep.

She never visited Richard's and Mavis's home again. They often asked her and she sometimes thought she would like to go, but was kept back by a feeling that, on her last visit, Mrs Brownlow had looked on her as an intruder. Every month or two Richard and Mavis would come to Heatherley for a weekend, or Richard would come alone on a Sunday and return the same night. Their walks and talks went on and they still delighted in each other's company, but there was a slight, indefinable change in their relationship, a shadow, the shade of a shade, had crept between them. Her friends, as she had expected, were sorry when she told them she had given up the attempt to pass the examination that was to have brought her to live near them, and when she tried to explain the motives which lay at the root of her decision she was told, for the first time in her life, though not the last, that she cared more for places than people. And it was no good her trying to get them to laugh it off by saying that she had been a cat in a previous existence and that it was always places not persons to which cats were attached, for they were really grave and a little hurt. And it hurt Laura to know she had disappointed them. However, one article of their belief which they had frequently rehearsed and Richard now repeated was that we all have to live our own lives and must be left free to make our own decisions. After a little more discussion the subject of Laura's projected promotion to town was dropped. But the slight shadow remained, and on Laura's side the feeling that, between herself and her friends, all was not quite as it had been.

Then, one winter evening when it had been dark for hours and Laura, already muffled up for a dash for home through the darkness and cold, was locking the post-office door on the inside, she was surprised to see through the glass upper panel Richard standing outside on the pavement. Against the dark background of the unlighted street, with the faint rays of the office oil-lamp falling upon it, his face looked unnaturally pale. His coat collar was turned up against the cold, which made him look hunched up and dejected; but he smiled his old smile when he saw her and signalled to her to make haste and come out, and the first words he said when she had come round from the back of the house were, "I want to talk to you."

She had nowhere indoors to take him to talk. Her room, having a bed in it, was out of the question at that date, and her landlady's front room, which she sometimes borrowed when she had friends to tea, would not be available with no previous notice. So they walked off through the village and out on the main road. The weather that night was depressing; there had been snow which the raw, cold thaw was rapidly turning to slush; fog made the darkness darker, and the few people they met were obviously hurrying home. They alone were making for the open country.

Mavis had been unwell with a cough left behind by one of the chest colds to which she was subject and one of Laura's first questions was "How is Mavis?"

"Not at all well," he said, "that is one of the things I want to tell you about", and, after Laura had said how sorry she was, not another word was spoken until they reached the crossroads. Then he felt for her arm, and as they moved slowly along the main road, enclosed and cut off from the rest of the world by a curtain of mist, Richard told Laura that Mavis had been examined by a doctor who had told their Aunt Maggie that, although there was no positive symptom of the disease, he felt he ought to warn her that her niece's condition showed a marked tendency to tuberculosis. She certainly ought not to remain in London this cold, foggy weather. He supposed the South of France was out of the question? Ah, yes, of course, he knew something of the family circumstances. Then some sheltered place in the south of this country, Bournemouth, perhaps, or Shanklin.

"Oh, poor, poor Mavis!" cried Laura, appalled, "and just as she was doing so well in her new post! Isn't she terribly disappointed—and frightened?"

"Disappointed, of course, but not at all frightened. Says it's all nonsense, the doctor has made a mistake; except for a bit of a cough, no worse than she has had other winters, she feels perfectly well. At first she flatly refused to be packed off, as she calls it, to Bournemouth."

"But she is going?"

"Going? Of course she's going," he said, and he went on to explain that such symptoms as those the doctor had discovered in Mavis were taken seriously nowadays and had to be dealt with at once, while there was still ground for hope that the patient would throw them off entirely. There were sanatoriums where rich patients were sent, where they lived practically in the open air and were placed on a diet, and homes for the poor who were similarly affected were being established all over the country. Even fairly advanced cases, he said, responded to the new treatment, and there had been some almost miraculous cures. Laura, who had read all this in the newspapers, and felt sure that Mavis would recover—she must!—knew also that a long stay at Bournemouth or Shanklin would be expensive. "And it can be managed?" she asked.

He then told her that their Aunt Maggie had a little money of her own, not enough for her to live upon, but the interest brought her in a few shillings a week, enough for her clothes and personal expenses, and after her talk with the doctor she had determined to realise sufficient of her small capital to give Mavis three months at Bournemouth. Aunt Maggie had a friend there, a trained nurse, who kept a boarding-house for delicate people, many of whom came there in winter, and Aunt Maggie had written to this friend and arrangements had been made to place Mavis under her care.

"I hate taking her money from her," he said, "it's robbing the widow of her mite; but what can I do? I've been able to save nothing. Though, in any case, Mavis would have gone there. She's going to have the best possible treatment, if I have to borrow the money from a moneylender. I've often been tempted to borrow from one in the past and may come to it yet. One day you'll read in the newspaper, 'Young man in moneylender's clutches!' and you'll find you know that young man. Oh, Laura, you don't know, you will never know, what I have gone through. I've been like someone trying to climb up out of a pit who, every time he came near the top, was knocked on the head and fell back to the bottom again. And so it will always be with me. I can never marry, you know that, don't you, Laura?"

Laura stiffened inwardly. Some mean little spirit said in her heart, "Good Heavens! surely he doesn't think I want him to marry me!" but another voice which was also her own told her it was no time for silly pride, and she said, as lightly as she was able, "But you don't want to marry anyone, do you? And perhaps by the time you do you'll have made a fortune."

Pacing to and fro, enclosed in the fog, Richard opened his heart to Laura as never before. He spoke of their happy home life when Mavis and he were children; of how fine and generous a man his father had been; his mother, how gay and charming; of their seaside holidays, their Christmas parties, and of all the other pleasures he had shared with his little sister. Then of the sudden blow which had put an end to his happy, carefree youth and brought him, all unprepared, face to face with a man's responsibilities. He said the few friends who had rallied round them in their trouble, business friends of his father and their wives, had told him he was wonderful, that very few youths of his age could have acted as he did, but he himself had known all the time that, far from being wonderful, he was but a poor sort of creature. He had sometimes cried into his pillow at night, "blubbered" was the word he used; "I blubbered like a kid when an unexpected bill came in, or a letter came from mother saying she hated her new treatment; or, if nothing of that kind had happened, I lay sweating with fear lest the next day should bring some demand upon me to which I was unequal. Mavis never knew this, no one knew it, I always managed somehow to keep up my spirits before others, and Mavis herself was truly wonderful, you should have seen her down on her knees scrubbing the scullery, or counting the pennies left in her purse when she had been shopping, without a word of complaint—did I say without complaint? So far from it that she would make fun out of what must have been hardships. Oh, my poor Mavis!"

Laura told him, as any other comforter would, that he was feeling so discouraged because this latest trial had followed so many other trials and followed them when, at last, they had seemed at an end. He must try to take this new trouble separately. Mavis would recover, of course she would; indeed, the doctor had not found anything definitely wrong with her: he had advised that she should winter in a warmer climate merely as a precaution. Mavis had wonderful spirit, he had just said so himself, and Laura knew it too. In the mild, pine-scented air of Bournemouth she would soon throw off her cough and grow stronger, and in six months' time he would look back on his fears of tonight as part of a nightmare.

When he had become more cheerful and hopeful they parted, for he had at last agreed to Laura's suggestion that he should leave her at the crossroads and take a shorter and more direct way to the railway station than the one through Heatherley. By doing so he would catch the ten-thirty train and so secure some of the rest he needed before going to his work in the morning.

Still enveloped in the fog, they stood beneath the signpost, her hand in his hand. All had been said that could be said and their few moments' silence was filled by the sound of water dripping, *drip, drip,* from the boughs, and the humming of telegraph wires. Then, to relieve the tension, Laura said, without much thought, "I suppose it will be some time before I see you again?" and he answered, very sadly, "I'm afraid it will, Laura. There will be no holidays for me, not even weekends, until Mavis is better."

They parted and she stood for a few seconds listening to his retreating footsteps. Then the sound ceased for a moment; he turned and came back at a running pace, but all he had to say when he reached her under the signpost was a last "Good-bye, Laura".

Mavis went home from Bournemouth apparently restored to her usual health. Her post in the City had been filled during her absence and she found one, less exacting, as secretary to a lady in Surrey. It was such a post as is seldom found in real life, with light work in luxurious surroundings. Her employer was an unmarried woman, a writer of stories for children, who, living alone except for a houseful of servants, wanted a secretary who would also be a companion. Mavis was taken for carriage drives and had the run of a beautiful garden and well-stocked library and had plenty of leisure to enjoy them. The one disadvantage of her position was that she had no regular, specified whole days off and could seldom go home; but even for this there was promised compensation in the way of long holidays whenever her employer was travelling abroad. The time for that had gone for that year, but she had one week at home during the summer and, for the weekend, came with Richard to Heatherley. That time theirs was a farewell visit, for Laura was leaving Heatherley to take up a post fifty miles farther from London. They would have no more weekends together, but Richard and Mavis planned to spend some part of their future summer holidays near Laura's new abode.

As it turned out, the three friends never met again. Mavis's cure had not been complete and she spent the next winter at one of the new sanatoriums. While she was there Laura heard from her often and her letters were teeming with fun and fancy and brimming with affection. She still would not believe that there was anything serious the matter with her and declared that she was getting all this attention, 'petting' she called it, under false pretences. Laura had also letters from Richard. His were not so gay as those of Mavis, though he was no longer as despondent as he had been at the onset of her illness.

Mavis again recovered and went back to her post in Surrey, and Laura heard with delight that her kind employer had promised to take her with her to winter in Rome. Later, there were letters and picture postcards from Italy, and once, a long flat basket of glorious spring flowers came by post from the French Riviera.

Then, gradually, the letters which passed between Laura and her two friends grew fewer and farther apart. Time and distance are great separators, especially when, as in this case, they are aided by circumstances. Laura still wrote to and heard from Richard occasionally up to the time of her marriage, when the correspondence ceased. But though separated from her friends and plunged deep into the absorption of living her own life, Laura never forgot or ceased to be grateful to them for the happiness they had once brought into her life, and the time she had spent in their company came to signify to her in retrospect the high-water mark of her youth.

What happened to Mavis she never knew. It is to be feared that that bright, high-spirited young life was not a long one. Of Richard she did hear once more. Many years after he and Mavis had passed out of her life, Laura's youngest son, then an engineering apprentice, passed to her over the supper-table one of his technical journals for her to look at the illustration of a new liner which had just been launched, and there, on turning the page, she read an account of a presentation to Richard on his retirement from the service of the cable company.

A portrait of the once familiar face looked up at her from the page. It was that of a prosperous, kindly-looking middle-aged man, clean-shaven and a little inclined to plumpness; but the eyes which gazed straight out of the portrait at the beholder were Richard's eyes, keen, steadfast, and slyly humorous, and the smile on the lips was Richard's old smile.

According to the letterpress which accompanied the portrait he had had a distinguished career. He had been on the company's business for some years in China, and other sojourns of his in the Far East were mentioned. He appeared to be still unmarried, for there was no mention of a Mrs Richard Brownlow, and the farewell gift of his colleagues, instead of taking the form of a piece of plate for domestic use, was a portfolio of old prints, of which, it was stated, he already possessed a notable collection. Mention was made of the cottage on the east coast where it was hoped he would spend many years of well-earned retirement, "with his books, antique furniture and old prints about him". A wish that found an echo in one reader's heart, mingled with some regret that their ways in life had been so far asunder.

The Village in Wartime

The outbreak of the Boer War was a stirring event to a people who for two generations had been involved only in minor warfare with those described by Kipling as 'lesser breeds without the Law'. The elderly, of course, remembered the Crimean War. Veterans of that war still came to cottage doors hawking bootlaces, or were seen pushing barrel organs about the streets. Others, with pensions, had settled in neat little cottages and were still fighting their battles over again in fancy upon benches they shared with other elders on village greens, or by alehouse fires. Laura herself knew several of these, and she also knew a quiet little white-haired old lady who had been one of Miss Nightingale's nurses. But that war had been over long before the majority of those living at the end of the century had been born and to those of the younger generation it was as much a matter of history as the Battle of Hastings.

When the new, exciting conflict broke out in South Africa it was welcomed with flag-waving and other rejoicings. For some time stories had been appearing in the newspapers of diamond merchants and other business men of British nationality being insulted and, in some cases, suffering personal violence at the hands of the original settlers on the Rand. "The cheek of it! The confounded cheek of it! It's as good as an insult to the British flag. We shall have to give these Boers a lesson, that's certain!" People living in sequestered English villages who had hitherto scarcely known of the existence of such a people suddenly acquired an intimate knowledge of the nature and habits of the Boers. They were filthy in their persons, addicted to brandy, shared their wives with any chance comer, let their hair and beards grow longer than was decent, and, above all, were wily. Their President Kruger, more familiarly known as Oom Paul, was pictured in newspaper cartoons as a huge, hideous old man brandishing a Bible in one hand and in the other a brandy bottle. That such a nation with such a president should dare to defy our Government made the ordinary Englishman's blood boil. "We've got to have a slap at them if only to put them in their place," was the general conclusion, often expressed with the rider, "The pity of it is that they'll cave in before our troops have time to get there."

Others, who from superior education and more exact information as to the events which had led up to the climax were better qualified to judge, rejoiced that, after long years of lethargy, our country was once more about to assert her authority as one of the greatest, some said *the* greatest, of world powers. We had been too modest, too lenient, they said, and see what had come of it; now, once for all, we must give such small upstarts a lesson. That done, no other small community would ever dare to endanger the peace of the world. It was really a war to prevent future wars.

There were, it is true, a few who maintained that the Boers were an honest, hardworking race of farmers who had as much right as those belonging to larger nations to manage their own affairs in their own way; and though doubtless they had been misled by their leaders in the present instance, they did not deserve half the obloquy which was being heaped upon them. These persons were known as pro-Boers and were most unpopular. The windows of their houses were smashed by stones after dark, boys called rude names after them in the streets and burned their effigies in bonfires. Down at Hayling Island the shrubs and flowers in Mr Stead's garden were uprooted and his garden roller was run out to sea. But, apart from such petty acts of mob violence, the pro-Boers were left severely alone. There was no 18B.[47] They were at liberty to express their opinions in public, as in private, if they could find listeners. Heatherley had its pro-Boer in the person of Mr Hertford's brother, who proclaimed his principles by growing a beard and wearing a wideawake hat, similar to those worn by the Boers in pictures. The only effect of his unpopular attitude was a mild sending to Coventry. Nobody who was not obliged to do so on business spoke to him in the street or visited him at his home; but, as one half of the villagers were employed by him and the other half employed him, this was scarcely noticeable. Neither those who looked to him for their weekly wages, nor those who had pipes liable to freeze and roof tiles which might need replacing at short notice, could afford to ignore him. Mr Hertford himself, rather surprisingly, had come out as an ardent supporter of the war, so the two brothers had plenty to argue about at their evening sessions.

The section of the general public with which Laura came most into contact were wholehearted supporters of the war. Few, indeed, expected it to affect them in any way personally. No young wife looked at her husband and no mother at her big schoolboy son with the unspoken prayer that the war might be over before their turn came to take part in it, for there was no conscription and no talk of conscription and it was supposed that, like previous wars, it would be fought to a finish by the standing Army. When, afterwards, volunteers were called for, the number required was comparatively small. All ordinary men had to do was to pay their taxes while their womenfolk rolled bandages, made shirts, and knitted socks for 'the Tommies', as the private soldiers were called. Men, women, and children alike waved flags, sang patriotic songs, and cheered the soldiers on to victory.

'Tommy', or 'Tommy Atkins', after years of being regarded as the dregs of society, suddenly became a hero. When the early contingents of the 'fifty thousand horse and men' set out for Table Bay, crowds lined the streets to see them march past. Tommy was

---

[47] Section 18B of the Defence of the Realm Act, which in the Second World War allowed arrest and internment of those believed to be sympathetic to enemy powers

dragged from the ranks to be kissed by strange girls, gifts of sweets and tobacco were showered upon him, and he was given the addresses of complete strangers wishing to boast the distinction of receiving a letter from the Front. Other crowds lined the quays to wave and cheer as his transport moved out to the strains of *The Soldiers of the Queen, Dolly Gray* or *The Girl I Left behind Me.*

Tons of white enamel buttons with portraits of the popular generals printed in colours were sold in the shops and worn as brooches or lapel ornaments. With the older people Lord Roberts led as first favourite; the younger generation favoured Baden-Powell, and Generals Buller and Kitchener had their supporters. Children let loose from school ran about shouting:

> Lord Roberts and Kitchener,
> Baden-Powell and White,
> All dressed in khaki, all going to fight,
> When we catch Kruger how happy we'll be,
> We'll have a tug at his whiskers and have a Jubilee.

That dashing new colour, the khaki of the soldiers' field uniforms, became the rage for women's coats and costumes. Red, white and blue striped bands were used to bring the somewhat outmoded sailor hat up to date. Concerts and other entertainments were got up, the proceeds to benefit the troops, and altogether, as one of the girls said, the time was thrilling. Women of all ages knitted comforts for the soldiers. Many had first to learn to knit, for knitted garments had long been out of fashion and the old, homely craft of knitting was almost a lost art. But all went to it with a will, and cargoes of khaki socks, scarves, kneecaps and Balaclava helmets were soon being despatched to the Front. Later on, soldiers invalided home reported that in some places the veldt was strewn for miles with these votive offerings which, though kindly meant, were less in demand in the South African climate than they had been in the frozen trenches before Sebastopol. The workers then concentrated on knitting socks and making shirts, which were more in demand. Laura's contribution to this movement was a long, wide scarf of scarlet wool, knitted on wooden needles, which she worked on behind the post-office counter. The colour of the wool was not her own choice, it had been provided by some organisation, and she had to repeat this many times to callers who had remarked that it would make a good mark "for one of these here snipers". It was her first piece of knitting since she had left off wearing homeknit wool stockings in the winter and she grew very tired of it before it was finished. Had anyone then told her how many miles of knitting she would do in her lifetime and what a great solace it would become to her she would not have believed them.

Another wartime occupation was making flags for decoration. Every victory, even the smallest, was celebrated at home. Every house put out at least one flag, the streets were festooned with bunting, and the village or town brass band was called out to play patriotic airs. The stock of flags on the market was soon exhausted and homemade flags had somehow to be contrived from lengths of red, white, and blue sateen. There was soon a shortage of material in those colours, and those fortunate enough to secure material for their flag or flags still had another difficulty to contend with, how to shape their work and blend the three colours to avoid solecism. On one occasion the rumour went round that a certain householder was flying the French flag. France was then regarded in this country as a potential enemy and those who were told that the French flag was floating over their village street were so horrified at the idea that several of them went to the house to expostulate with the offender. They found the report was true; the tricolour was indeed floating from the bedroom window of a respected old dressmaker who had never before been suspected of French sympathies. But it was hauled in with great haste when its maker was made aware of the enormity she had unwittingly perpetrated. "You'll be flying the Boer flag next, if you're not careful," she was told by a friendly critic.

As well as the victories there were reverses for our troops. Many and unlooked-for reverses, Laura learned afterwards, in the early months of the war. In this country at large, in better informed circles, one week of bad news which caused general depression was known as the Black Week. The intellectuals living in the neighbourhood no doubt shared this anxiety, but no depression was felt by the ordinary villagers; their confidence in our troops and their leaders never wavered for a moment. If the report of some set-back appeared in the newspapers, it was speedily explained as a 'dodge' of 'Bobs', or Buller, or White to deceive the enemy. Of the prolonged siege of Mafeking Laura heard one man say: "Our troops'll break out when they're ready, you'll see. Baden-Powell's only keeping 'em shut up to draw on them old Boers."

The calling-up of the Yeomanry and the forming of various volunteer regiments brought the war a little nearer home, though the number of families affected was still very small in proportion to the population. The majority of the volunteers were young, unattached men; farmers' sons and others who could already ride and shoot were supposed to be the most desirable recruits. But clerks and shopmen in towns also crowded the recruiting offices and at one time there were many of these stranded at Aldershot, unable to begin their training until horses could be procured. "My God," said one of these to Laura, "the bally old war'll be over before we even embark", and he looked so romantic in his new khaki uniform and smart slouch hat, turned rakishly up at one side, that Laura felt almost as sorry for him as he did for himself. But he and his comrade yeomen had ample time in which to get there and to see some hard fighting, for the war lasted three years, and soon the first question on meeting a friend was, "Have you anyone out at the Front?" The few, it was still but a few, who could answer "Yes" answered proudly.

With the appearance of the smarter looking Yeomen and City Imperial Volunteers [C.I.V.s] poor Tommy Atkins suffered an eclipse in popular esteem. In the country towns which had a Yeomanry Headquarters even the yeomen who had enlisted only for home defence were treated as heroes. Laura had one amusing little experience of this. In one of the war years, during her holidays, she went for a weekend to visit some friends living in a small Bedford-shire town and on the Sunday evening was taken to the railway station to witness the return from camp of the local Yeomanry troop.

What was, for such a small town, a huge crowd had gathered in the street leading to the railway station, not only of townspeople, but also many from neighbouring villages, and there was shouting and cheering and waving of hats and handkerchiefs when the train steamed in. The road was so choked with sightseers that it was only with difficulty that a stretcher-bearing party could force its way from the station entrance to a waiting ambulance; especially as, on the appearance of the stretcher, the crowd rushed forward in great excitement. "Good old Sergeant! Good old Sergeant!" was the cry, "Glad to see you safe home again, old fellow!" Then someone suggested, "Let's give him three times three," and the three times three was given and many times repeated.

Laura concluded that the prostrate warrior waving his hand weakly over the side of the stretcher had been invalided home from the Front, probably after distinguished service; but afterwards, when hoping for some story of heroism she enquired into the matter, she was told that the invalid was just an ordinary Home Defence man who had been ill in camp—with pork poisoning.

For the first few months of the war a small crowd gathered on Sunday mornings outside the post office to read and comment upon the bulletin of war news posted in the window, and "Any news?" was a frequent question at the post-office counter on other days. A few of the more prominent residents had private bulletins of war news telegraphed to them from London nightly, but the contents of these, like other telegraphic communications, were inviolable, and Laura, in possession of the very latest news, found these questions embarrassing until she invented the formula, "No *official* news", which satisfied everyone.

In those pre-broadcasting days many well-to-do country dwellers had the late news of any happening which stirred public interest telegraphed to them. Election results, the verdict in murder trials, closing prices on the Stock Exchange and other such matters. During the Rheims court-martial of Captain Dreyfus, a priest— judging by his appearance a Catholic priest, and by his accent a Frenchman—called every evening for a telegram addressed to him at the post office. Often his telegram would not have arrived and he would wait, sometimes for the better part of an hour, pacing to and fro on the pavement outside the door, or standing, a dark figure in the background, while others came and went about their business at the counter. No-one who came in appeared to know him or even to notice his presence and Laura had not seen him before and never saw him afterwards; but she never forgot his face and expression when, one evening towards the end of the trial, she noticed that the hand he held out for his telegram was trembling and that beads of perspiration stood upon his brow. She often wondered afterwards who he was, where he came from, and if he had any personal connection with those involved.

When known names began to appear in the casualty lists and men who had suffered from that scourge of the war, enteric fever, were invalided home, pale and emaciated, those who had friends or relatives serving overseas began to realise the grim reality of the war. Among those whose own lives were unaffected, enthusiasm declined. There was no food shortage or rationing or billeting of troops to remind people that there was a war on, and of course there were no evacuees, for no part of the homeland was threatened. Between the Relief of Ladysmith and that of Mafeking ordinary country people appeared to forget the war, or, if they thought or spoke of it, it was as something dragging on, far away in a foreign country, not as any great concern of their own.

Laura sometimes almost envied those people their detachment. She had had almost from the beginning 'someone out at the Front'. Her brother Edmund,[48] next in age to herself in her family and her childhood's playmate and closest friend, had, at the outbreak of war, been staying with some relatives in Yorkshire. He had enlisted at once as a regular soldier in the West Yorks Regiment and at barely nineteen years of age went overseas as one of a draft. Laura said goodbye to him on a snowy Sunday morning at Aldershot railway station. The train by which she had to travel back to Heatherley was an hour late, for the war and the snow together had upset the timetable, and they walked together up and down the cold platform, talking: she with the forced cheerfulness which marks all such partings; he, flushed with excitement and his blue eyes glowing with enthusiasm as he tried to impress upon her his great good luck in getting out with the draft.

He went gaily, for to him, nurtured as his spirit had been on the tales of old romance and chivalry they had devoured together as children, war was one of the greatest possible human adventures; one which he had never thought to see in his lifetime, but one in which now, as it seemed miraculously, he was to take part. But Laura was full of fears and misgivings. He looked so young and, as she thought, tender with his slight, boyish figure encased in ill-fitting wartime khaki, and she dreaded for him the hardships as well as the dangers of war.

They were practically alone on the platform, for the other passengers had crowded into the warmer waiting-rooms, and Edmund, after remarking on this, began to repeat one of their old favourite passages from Scott's poems. It was the Death of Marmion. Laura had loved that passage in childhood, but she loved it no longer. The very sound of the word 'death' made her heart feel cold as stone. But she managed to smile until the train pulled out and from the carriage window she had waved a long farewell to Edmund. Her last view was of him standing erect at the end of the platform, his hand raised to his forehead in a military salute. In the railway carriage she found other women and girls who had been to Aldershot on similar errands, and her silent tears were unnoticed in the general weeping and comparing of experiences.

---

[48] Edwin Timms

There followed for her days of anxiety and nights when she would lie awake picturing Edmund alone and wounded on the veldt. She never once imagined him dead, but always wounded and alone beneath the strange, bright stars he had written of in his letters. Actually, he came through his three years' service in South Africa without any serious injury, his destiny being to die in 1916 on a more fiercely contested battlefield. Once during his South African service he was taken prisoner while scouting and carried off by a party of Boer horsemen who at last, finding him an encumbrance, stripped him of all but trousers and shirt and abandoned him on the open veldt.

They had carried him miles into wild, desolate country on which the fierce sun poured down by day and the night air chilled to the bone. One of the horsemen, as they were riding off, had turned in the saddle and flung back to Edmund his water-bottle, but there was little water in it and he had no food. After many turnings and twistings, for he had little sense of direction, he did at last reach an English camp, steering by the sun by day and the stars by night. On the way he had but one adventure. His own store of water was soon exhausted; it was a waterless country and he was suffering agonies of thirst when, on the third day, he came to a Boer homestead, the first human habitation he had seen. No human being or domestic animal was in sight; there was no smoke from a fire, the only window he could see was boarded over, and he thought the place was deserted. But he could not be sure of that, and said afterwards that he loitered for what seemed hours in the vicinity, lurking behind tussocks and patches of scrub, afraid to approach the dwelling lest the men of the house should be hiding there. In his weak state he would easily have been overpowered, and yet he was so drawn towards the house by the pangs of thirst and the certainty that water must be there, that he found himself insensibly edging nearer.

Presently a Boer woman, coming round the corner of the house from the back, came face to face with him. She was old and stout and unkempt, the very image of old Nancy Baines, he said, naming an old woman at home; and like Nancy, she had a pleasant, good-natured expression. When she realised that the ragged, half-naked stranger was an enemy soldier, she naturally looked startled. But she did not spit at him or shout abuse, as the Boer women were said to do to their helpless and unarmed prisoners of war, and when he pointed to his baked lips and held out his water-bottle, she took the bottle and filled it. Not one word passed between them, for neither knew the language of the other, but human compassion and human gratitude can be expressed without words.

When Edmund, on reaching an English camp, told others of this incident to which, as he thought, he owed his life, he was told that the woman was probably alone in the house. The Boers left their old people to shift for themselves when they flitted, and being alone, she was of course afraid to offend one who might prove troublesome. But Edmund himself did not accept that explanation. He firmly believed that the woman had acted from pure human kindness.

* * * * *

After his South African service Edmund's regiment was sent direct to India, where he served a further five years before returning to this country. Then, after a year or two at home, he emigrated to Canada. He had been on the eve of emigrating there when the war broke out and he had enlisted. Had not the war and his long foreign service intervened he would have begun life in his new country as a boy of eighteen with the vigour and adaptability of youth; when he actually went it was as a man of thirty who had seen something of the world and who, had it been possible, would have preferred to settle down at home. He still loved the land and wished for nothing better than to spend the rest of his life working on it; but to farm on his own account without capital was impracticable, and the wage of a farm labourer at that time was not a living wage. Being unmarried, he had managed to live fairly comfortably at home on his earnings during the interval, but even he, the least ambitious of men in a worldly sense, had realised at last that, if he was to live a full life, he must go further.

Laura had married early in the century and her new home[49] was a hundred miles from that of their childhood; she had her house and a young family to care for, and during all those years she saw her brother but once. That was when she spent a few days with her children at her old home a fortnight before Edmund emigrated. During the short time they spent together Laura was much taken up with the care of her children, Edmund was working on a farm and did not return till evening, and they had but one walk and confidential talk together. Then they had been, late in the evening, to see a younger sister off by train from the nearest town. It was September, a moist, dark night of soft winds blowing over the

---

[49] Winton, Bournemouth

stubble of the stripped fields, and they took their return walk of three miles easily, once talking themselves to a standstill by the roadside pond into which Laura had fallen through the ice when a child. As they stood there, talking of this and that, of their childhood days and some of the queer old characters they had known; of Edmund's travels (York Minster and the Taj Mahal were the sights which had most impressed him), and of Laura's home and children—somewhere, a field or two away in the darkness, a man's voice was suddenly uplifted in song.

"Old Buffy," said Edmund, "going home by the fieldpath and singing to keep up his spirits in the dark." The old country songs were no longer heard there and the one old Buffy was singing was but a popular music-hall song of the moment, but he had a pleasant voice and the soft, warm darkness lent enchantment. The brother and sister stood, listening and savouring the good earthy smells of the fields. Then, as they turned to go, Edmund said, waving his arm to include the fields and trees and hedgerows they both knew so intimately, "I've seen a good bit of the world, but I've seen nothing I liked better than this. It takes some beating. Yes, it takes some beating." Laura said, "Yes, I know how you feel. Other places are richer and finer and more exciting to see, but to us, this is somehow more satisfying—more real—more solid—it has the goodness of bread."

Edmund liked his new life in a new country and his friends thought he had settled there for life; but a year or two later he was back in England, again a soldier, and on his way to his last war. He had one short home leave early in 1916, but at the time Laura's children were down with whooping cough and she was unable to go to their old home to see him. Although it was March the weather was wintry, snow lay over the whole country, and the night Edmund set out on his return journey to the trenches in France the Oxfordshire roads were barely passable. But when duty calls a soldier must obey and Edmund shouldered his pack and rifle and went down the old path from his mother's cottage, "loaded up like a horse", as she said afterwards.

He had no-one of his own kin young enough or strong enough to accompany him to the railway station, but a kind neighbour volunteered to see him off and to help him on the way with his baggage. He stayed with him till near midnight at the station, waiting for the overdue train; then, having the long tramp back through the snow before him and fearing his wife might be anxious, he wished

Edmund goodbye and good luck and left him alone in the fireless waiting-room. The train, as it turned out, was not running, the line was blocked with snow and the night of that freezing vigil was the last the soldier was ever to spend in his own beloved country. Three weeks later he was killed in action.

The morning on which Laura heard of his death was one of glorious April sunshine. Larks were singing above her suburban garden and she noticed as she shook out the crumbs from the breakfast-cloth that the lilac was budding. Her children had recovered from their illness and she was rejoicing that her troubles were over and that summer was coming, when the letter arrived. It was one of her own letters to Edmund, returned to her, marked in pencil, "Killed in Action", the first intimation of his death because the official letter which should have told of it had been misdirected.

Returned to her with her letter was a broadsheet copy she had sent enclosed in it of Wordsworth's *Happy Warrior*, and she came to feel in later life that in the matter of his death Edmund was indeed happy, for he was a soldier by his own choice and he died a soldier's death on the battlefield. Unlike some who fall in warfare, he had not to relinquish life before he had well tasted it, and unlike others, he left behind him no brood of young children to face the world fatherless. He went the way of the old heroes of his childhood, in the prime of his manhood, fighting for a cause he wholeheartedly believed in, and went swiftly and suddenly in the heat of a battle, a happy warrior.

* * * * *

The Boer War ended, and again there were scenes of rejoicing, but rejoicings of a quieter and more sober kind than the outbreak of almost delirious joy which had distinguished Mafeking night. For the war had proved more serious and lasted longer than people had anticipated. It had brought anxiety and bereavement to some families and, to all, a depression of spirits, changes in the way of living, increased taxation, the rise in prices inseparable from war. When at last the long-drawn-out struggle ended in victory for our troops there was heartfelt rejoicing, but it was a rejoicing best expressed by the frequently heard exclamation, "Thank God it's over!"

At Heatherley, when the news came through, flags were flown, people wore red, white and blue rosettes in their buttonholes, cheers were heard in the streets and the public houses did a brisker business than usual; but beneath this surface gaiety people were more thoughtful than they had been at the outbreak of war. A local landowner with a fine estate had lost both his heir and his only other son, and from two or three humbler homes in the district one member of the family had gone overseas in the flower of his youth to return no more. Life, people told each other, would never be quite the same again. Of course there would be no more war in their lifetime. For one thing, this war had been a lesson to the world, and for another, in future not many nations would be inclined to face the cost of a war. Look at the cost of the one now ended, thousands of pounds a day! And how prices had risen, all due to the war, it was said; though why eggs laid and eaten in the same parish should go up threepence a dozen was a mystery that most speakers declared was beyond them.

Fortunately it was also beyond them to see into the future or to know that the war so recently ended was but as the first faint tremor presaging an earthquake.

The New Century

The old century waned. "It came in with wars and it's going out with a war," people reminded each other, not pessimistically but hopefully, for there was a general idea that the war then in progress would be the last war. If not peace over the whole earth, it was confidently expected that there would be permanent peace wherever British influence extended.

And the new century would bring other blessings. The old century had been a marvellous one. Look at the new inventions! Look at the progress! they said as they counted their blessings— railway travelling, the telephone and the telegraph, even the humble bicycle. And the march of civilisation, the putting down of the slave trade, free State education for children, the reform of prisons and criminal laws, the advance in science and medicine. Why, at the

152

beginning of the century they hadn't any chloroform even, and people had to lie and look on while their legs were sawn off! In the year 1800 a child of ten or twelve might be hanged for stealing a few apples, and until well into the century even younger children were working in factories and in dark underground mines. The nineteenth century had altered all that; it remained to be seen what new and astonishing developments the twentieth would unfold.

That the developments would proceed along much the same lines nobody doubted. The newspapers foretold that our exports, already stupendous, would continue to increase and that higher wages and a better standard of living for the masses would follow; that there would be new and still more marvellous mechanical inventions which would relieve man of the necessity of working more than two or three hours a day. As well as these material advantages, it was hinted that a new era of human happiness was at hand. People were going to live longer and healthier lives, science would see to that, and extended leisure would provide an opportunity for mental and spiritual cultivation. That a new century would bring a new and better way of living was taken for granted.

People began to look forward to the exact moment when the change would begin. Did the old century end with the year 1899, or with 1900? There was a good deal of controversy on that point, and although the authorities decided that not until midnight on December 31st 1900 would the new and better time begin, general opinion inclined to the earlier date. Both New Year's Eves were kept by their respective supporters with more than ordinary festivity. Children of families, down to the youngest who could be supposed to comprehend the importance of the occasion, were allowed to stay up to see in the new century, for, as their parents told them, even they, young as they were, could not hope to see another such New Year's Day.

The first notable event of the new century was a sad one. In January 1901 it became known that the revered, beloved old Queen Victoria was failing in health, and on the twenty-second of that month she died. The nation was touched to the heart. People of mature age went about with tears in their eyes, saying, "Our poor old Queen! We shall never see her like on the throne of this country again!" On the gloomy January morning when the news of her death reached Heatherley many who had never before made any show of their loyalty mourned for the queen sincerely. Early in the day a poor working man, a fish hawker, came into the post office. "This is sad news about our queen," he said, and astonishingly, there were tears in his eyes. "What's Hecuba to him, or he to Hecuba, that he should weep for her?" asked Laura, as the door closed behind him, and then felt ashamed of her levity when she saw that Alma's big blue eyes were brimming over. For a day or two there were many such incidents, not always, not often tearful but always expressive of sincere personal sorrow. Faces were sad and voices grew tender as callers spoke of the nation's great loss and retold the many little stories current which illustrated the goodness of nature of her whom they spoke of as Victoria the Good, the Mother of her People.

Then the new king. When the war had begun there had been a queen on the throne; when it ended, as it must soon end, there would be a king. This perfectly natural circumstance, for at the outbreak of war the queen was of course a very old lady, had for many people an almost mystical significance. Kings had hitherto, to the vast majority of those then living in this country, been but names in history, part of the romance of past ages; and now to have a living king, and another Edward, on the throne was an exciting experience. And, all in good time, there would be a coronation. That was an event very few then living could remember, but upon which all could speculate.

But now, first of all, there was mourning for the queen to be contrived, for the whole nation went into mourning dress, probably for the last time in history. Women of means ordered new all-black outfits; those whose means did not permit this expense ransacked their wardrobes for something black to wear, a less vain quest than it would be now, since in those days mourning was worn for quite distant relatives and most women had by them relics of the last funeral they had attended. The very poor looked to their patrons for discarded black garments, or failing these, home-dyed their own clothes or sewed on to them bows of black crêpe. Only the gipsies, of whom there were many living on the heaths around Heatherley, were seen wearing bright colours. They were indeed more colourful than usual in their dress, for they reaped a rich harvest in cast-offs of the suddenly unfashionable red, blue and green shades which the original possessors decided it was no good keeping, as the styles would be hopelessly out of date before their new black was discarded.

For the first three months after the death of the queen only the attire of the gipsies provided a splash of colour in the gloom; then, as the days lengthened and brightened, black and white mixtures and soft tones of mauve and grey began to appear. Finally, women's dress that year went purple. Wine, plum, pansy, heather and lavender shades were in great demand. Traders sent their goods still in the piece and capable of taking such shades to the dye-vats, but a great stock of piece-goods, as well as made-up garments acquired before the general mourning, was left on their hands, and many of them went bankrupt. It was probably due to the representations of the traders, as well as to her own kind thoughtfulness, that when King Edward died, Queen Alexandra issued a communication asking the women of the nation not to go to the unnecessary expense of buying new mourning. A black tie or a black sleeveband for men and a black hat or scarf for women would, she said, be a sufficient outward sign of the sincere grief which she knew the loyal, affectionate hearts of his subjects felt for the loss of their beloved king.

The general public deferred to her wish; the more readily because, by the end of the first decade of the century, private and family mourning had become greatly modified. It was becoming rarer every year to see in the streets a man whose all-black suit, deep crêpe hatband and black kid gloves proclaimed a recent bereavement, or a woman enveloped in crêpe, from the deep band of that fabric on the bottom of her black skirt to the crêpe bows and crêpe flowers on her headgear. Black-bordered pocket-handkerchiefs were less in demand than they had been, and although black-bordered stationery was still in use the black border had narrowed considerably. Laura could remember the time when some mourning envelopes were so heavily bordered with black that only a square of white about the size of a visiting card was left in the middle for the address. Jet ornaments for mourning had also disappeared. Relatives of those whose death (with address) had been announced in the newspapers no longer received by post, from too-enterprising vendors, little boxes containing jet brooches and buckles and lockets and chains with the request that they would kindly choose what they required and remit the cost, plus postage. The only survival from the old-time deep mourning was the widow's bonnet, a close-fitting affair with a soft white ruche to frame the face and long crêpe streamers behind; and that, some unkind people said, only remained in favour because it was extraordinarily becoming to most women.

When Queen Victoria died the war was still in progress, and when in 1902 peace was declared, great regret was expressed that she had not lived to see that day. "It do seem hard she's not here to see the troops come home," said one of her humbler subjects, "'my troops' she used always to call 'em, always *my* troops, and she used to grieve over the casualty lists as if every one of the fallen had been her own child. Not that she was ever daunted, mind you; no, never not even when things were not going too well. 'I've got perfect confidence in my troops', she'd tell her ladies, and so she had bless her! If she'd been young and a man she'd have been out there herself at the head of 'em. Ah, she was a fine-spirited one, was our dear old queen!"

Stories were told of Queen Victoria and simple people continued to revere her memory right up to the outbreak of the world war in 1914. Then, after that great upheaval had subsided, her figure became obscured in the miasma of so-called Victorianism. Recently she has become to many of the younger generation the Queen Victoria of the film with that title. A few months ago Laura went into a small second-hand furniture shop to purchase a copy she had seen in the window of Nicholson's drawing of the Queen and found, in the course of conversation with the young girl who attended to her, that she had not recognised the subject of the picture. When told that it was Queen Victoria, she said, "Oh, is it?" then, after examining critically the aged figure which, with no outer trappings of royalty, was yet unmistakably royal, she said, "It's not a patch on what she was like in the film."

When Queen Victoria died, film entertainments in this country were in an experimental, tentative stage. No-one as yet dreamed that the cinematograph, as it was still called in full, would ever become overwhelmingly popular. There were so far no palatial buildings devoted entirely to film entertainments; one film was shown here and there, between music-hall turns or in the course of other entertainments. Laura saw her first film at Halstead, Essex, in 1898. It was billed as a 'Moving picture' and was entitled 'Night and Morning', or 'Morning and Night', the morning scene being of a wedding party coming out of church and the night scene was one of the bride performing a kind of a strip-tease act in a bedroom while the bridegroom peered round the edge of a screen, the whole moving in a flickering jig which dazzled the eyes of the beholders. During or immediately after the exhibition an elderly man stood up in the body of the hall to protest that the subject was not a seemly one "with ladies present". By the rest of the audience the film was accepted as a novelty, a freak turn. "It's a bit of a puzzle how they make the figures move," was the general comment upon it afterwards. No one then present dreamed that they had witnessed the first stumbling steps of a young art which was to become the most popular and the most remunerative of all arts in the twentieth century.

After the Boer War ended prosperity returned, and for a few years it seemed that the long-looked-for new era had begun. In society circles gaiety reigned. Accounts of opera nights, fancy-dress balls, dinners and garden parties, with lists of names of the distinguished persons present and a full description of the women's dresses and jewels, filled whole columns of the popular newspapers. About that time there were several divorce cases in high life and of these full, unbowdlerised reports appeared in print, to the delight, if not the edification of the average reader. For such news the appetite of the great public appeared to be insatiable in the days before fiction, as depicted on the films, made real life appear insipid. Picture postcards of society and stage beauties also helped to fill the void.

Before great houses in the West End when crimson carpets were laid from front door to curb and strains of dance music floated from brilliantly lighted interiors, a knot of women and girls would gather, like moths round a candle, to watch the arrival of the guests. "O-ooh! isn't she lovely!" "Isn't he handsome!" "Did you see her pearls? and her white velvet cloak trimmed with swansdown?" "What price that old dowager with the tiara?" "How'd you fancy yourself in an ermine cape, Nell?" they would ask each other un-enviously, tapping their feet on the pavement the while to the strains of *The Blue Danube*. The outdoor spectators would tire and go home. Most of them had to be up early to go to work the next morning. But the dance would go on until after sunrise, when the early milkman would thread with his barrow between departing carriages.

Dirt, squalor, crime and disease lurked, as it were, just round the corner, for the London slums were very much worse than they are today. From homes only a street or two distant from some of those mansions children went barefoot, dirty, ragged and hungry to school. Women in those terrible tenements sank into an aimless, effortless apathy, or made matters still worse than they would have been by taking to gin-drinking. Men were in and out of prison as a regular feature of their lives. The few individuals who stood firm and preserved their self-respect in such an environment did so by such an effort that they became aged and broken in health while they should still have been in their prime. Everyone knew that this was so. It was said daily that the slums were a blot on the civilisation of the twentieth century. Some of those very dancers went in for what they called 'slumming', visiting the poor in their homes, organising clubs for girls, raising money by bazaars and entertainments to send children for country holidays and in other ways to alleviate suffering. The women of Laura's own class sewed garments for slum children, in turn with those intended to clothe the heathen. But with the exception of a few noble men and women who devoted their lives to the present betterment and the future abolition of such conditions, no one felt any personal responsibility.

Certainly no one that Laura knew, of her own class and condition, felt more than a vague pity for those living in slums. If pressed to state their opinion on the subject they would say that, sad as such things were, they were inevitable. There had always been rich and poor and there always would be. Some would go further and say that when people sank to that state it was due to some fault in their own characters. Rather, it appeared, like the poor old horse in *Childe Roland to the Dark Tower came*— "He must be wicked to deserve such pain". Even those few who felt such things more deeply had no idea that they themselves might do or say something to alter them, for the power of public opinion was as yet imperfectly understood and the conscience of the individual as a component of the nation was unawakened.

Of the two extremes of the social scale Laura had little personal knowledge. Rich and fashionable people sometimes came into the post office and she saw that as a general rule they were pleasant to look at, that they had charming manners and moved with an easy negligence and general air of being at home in a world they found thoroughly agreeable. She knew they were not free from their share of human suffering, that anxiety, illness and bereavement touched them as they touched others, and from her own inside knowledge she knew that, at such times and in such circumstances, they were humanly vulnerable. But of their everyday lives and their attitude to life as a whole she knew nothing. Neither had she any personal knowledge of the lives of those belonging to what was then known as the depressed, or submerged, class. She knew the farm workers and their families among whom she had been born and bred; but they were a race apart, a survival of the old English peasantry, still living by the stern old peasant standards of self-help, thrift, and unremitting labour. "Living," as they said themselves, "where some might have starved", and in spite of poverty and hardship making a good job of that living. No one included them when speaking of the depressed classes. No one not directly concerned spoke or thought of them at all, except as an animate part of the country scenery.

Of the fashionable world and the underworld, Laura knew little but what she had read. The great middling mass of the people, especially those slightly above the poverty line, she knew intimately as one of themselves. And for them, during the early years of the century, higher wages, though partly countered by higher prices, created an atmosphere of prosperity. It was exhilarating to handle and help circulate money, even if one were very little better off in reality. And there were new ways in which money could be spent—on machine-made, mass-produced furniture, on cheap, ready-made clothes of fashionable cut, and the bewildering array of new grocery products—peaches and pineapples in tins, brought from the ends of the earth to figure on the Sunday tea-table, egg-saving custard powders, tinned fish and tinned meat, sauces and coffee extracts in bottles.

In towns the new threepenny and sixpenny stores provided an inexpensive shopping centre. There, to the strains of gramophone music, the housewife could spend a whole afternoon, circling round and round the different counters with her friends and finishing up with a cup of tea and a cake which cost but a copper or two. Though they admitted that many useful things could be found there, some of the older housewives said that a good deal of money was wasted; others that the blare of the music, the cheap, showy goods, and the surging of the crowds confused them. They liked a quiet life, they said, and preferred to do their shopping where the shop people knew them and would see they got what they wanted. "But", would exclaim some friend or neighbour of the new school, "how can you possibly know what you want before you see what's there?"—and in such remarks lay the clue to the old and the new attitudes to life. People who had formerly desired only such things as they needed were, under the influence of the new system of trading, learning to desire whatever was brought to their notice.

In country places new village halls were built where the villagers could meet for dances and whist drives, choral society practices, sewing parties and cookery lectures. Women were no longer cloistered in their homes. There were scholarships for village schoolchildren, and a little later Old Age Pensions for the aged. The agricultural labourers' wages went up from ten to fifteen shillings a week.

On Sundays village churches were no longer as well filled as they had been. In some parishes the clergyman reinstated the old ways of worship and was supported by a small but ardent band of worshippers; but these, though enthusiastic, were but a small portion of the inhabitants. In other parishes the clergyman took a leading part in the secular social life of his village, sitting on Parish Councils, organising clubs and sports and mutual-aid schemes, and good work was done in that way. But very few of the clergy preached to full churches or had much influence over their parish as a whole, for a common faith no longer knit old and young, rich and poor, into one family and the church was no longer the centre of village life. The new centre for the surrounding villages was the nearest town.

The motor-bus had not yet appeared, but there were horse buses, and there was the bicycle. People could reach in half an hour the goal which had previously called for an hour and a half of hard walking, and reach it not already tired out from the exertion of walking after their day's work, but fresh for the fun. The lighted shops, the jostling crowds, the sights, sounds and smells of a town appeared to have a fascination for those of the younger generation of country people. A little cheap shopping, a street-corner meeting or a band playing were added attractions, but failing these, they appeared quite content to stroll up and down the High Street in twos and threes until it was time to catch the bus or to mount their bicycles and go home. To these the public houses had little appeal. Hard drinking was already out of date and by the middle of the first decade of the new century the sight of a drunken man in the streets was becoming rare. What the country people chiefly enjoyed on their trips to town were the lights and the noise; above all, the sensation of being one of a crowd.

The Heatherley people shared such benefits as came their way. For a year or two after the turn of the century more money came into the village; the villagers dressed better, had more amusements, wider ideas and a better time generally. Some building was done and many looked forward to seeing in their own lifetime their village develop into a kind of garden city.

But Heatherley was not destined to develop into a town, or even to increase in size and prestige as a village. The neighbouring settlement was more at the heart of the district, nearer the hotels and large houses set in the choicest part of the hilly scenery which had always been the chief attraction to visitors, and more than a mile nearer a railway station. It was there the development took place. More houses were built, more shops opened; and when the inhabitants petitioned for a post and telegraph office nearer their homes the petition was granted. The place then became self-sufficient and Heatherley was left on the outer edge of the favoured area from which for a few years it had drawn a temporary importance. Apart from considerations of distance, the few shops there could not compete with the newer and more luxurious ones in the sister settlement. With better and more plentiful accommodation nearer the centre of things, visitors to the Heatherley apartment houses and cottage rooms became few, and those few were not of the well-paying kind. The day after the new telegraph office was opened the number of telegrams sent and received at Heatherley went down 80 per cent.[50] Laura's services were no longer needed; there was not sufficient work to keep her employed, and the postmaster's official remuneration in the new scheme of things barely allowed for Alma's smaller salary. So, as soon as arrangements could be made, Laura left Heatherley, as she then thought for ever, transferring herself to another post office in a distant part of the county. A few months later she was married.[51]

---

[50] 15th Sept 1900: 'Initial telegraph work at Hindhead was 60 telegrams per day, and it has considerably relieved the strain which hitherto existed at the Grayshott post office'—*Haslemere Herald*

[51] Married to John Thompson on 7th January 1903

Post-war Pilgrimage

When, twenty years after she had left Heatherley, Laura returned to live in that part of the country, the return was not of her own seeking but due to her husband's appointment as postmaster in the Heatherley district,[52] an appointment which might have been to any other place of the same size in the south of England. But although she had had no choice in the matter, the prospect of visiting her old haunts was a pleasing one, and once there, she took the earliest opportunity of walking over the heaths and through the woods to Heatherley.

She found the village little changed in appearance. The two short streets looked much as they had done, a little dustier and shabbier as to paint, with new names over many of the shop fronts

---

[52] Became postmaster at Liphook in August 1916

and the windows of what had been other shops, but were now private dwellings, covered with white lace curtains, but substantially the same. Madam Lillywhite's choice emporium had reverted to its old status; rolls of flannel and sheeting filled one of its windows, the other displayed saucepans, enamelled bowls and built-up pyramids of rolls of toilet paper. No building had been done in the centre of the village. Where the short length of pavement which ran before the post office and shops ended, the broken bank, which Laura remembered as left broken by the builder of the last house in the terrace, still crumbled peatily. The heather, surging up from the heath, broke over the bank and filled the air with the old honey-scent. Where there had been groups of pines between the clusters of buildings there were still groups of pines, and at the foot of the red trunks there were still pine-needle houses, made and stuck about with shards of pottery by children, though not by the same children who had played there when the century was new.

Laura discovered afterwards that on the side of the village nearest the more progressive settlement new roads had been built with houses of a suburban type. The other building sites, which in her time had been staked out in plots in accordance with ambitious plans on paper, had reverted to heath. Sites which had been intended for rows of houses and shops and big corner hotels were blotted out by a vigorous new growth of heather and gorse; bracken had sprung up and buried the curbs of prematurely made roads and only the bees were busy where it had been hoped that money, not honey, would be gathered. Heatherley had not developed according to plan. The march of progress had taken another direction. What new building there was had been centred around the big hotel on the hill and, while the sister settlement had spread and prospered, Heatherley had been left, still a small village, on the outer edge of the favoured district.

That afternoon Laura walked among the old familiar scenes like a ghost of the past. Very few people were in the streets of the village and of those few none knew or recognised her. The only one of them all she herself recognised was a shopkeeper standing at his door and stifling a yawn. When she had last seen him he had been young, slender and lively. During the interval he had become stout, bald, and apparently less lively. As he showed no sign of recognising her she passed on.

Then, as she turned a corner, Laura saw coming towards her the reporter of a local newspaper and thought "Ah, it's Tuesday!" for she remembered that Tuesday had been his day in the past for coming to Heatherley to collect such scraps of news as the place afforded. He was evidently then engaged in the same pursuit for he was walking, notebook in hand, in close converse with the village policeman.

That reporter[53] had been one of the friends of Laura's youth and there had been a time when he would even have risked losing an item of news for the sake of a talk with her. They had once shared a rather gruesome experience. After sitting side by side on the top bar of a sluice at the lakes laughing and talking for an hour one summer evening they had learned the next day that immediately after they left, the body of a drowned man had been taken from the water.[54] They had shared happier experiences, a primrosing expedition on Good Friday, an August Bank Holiday tramp over the moors, with stewed whortleberries and cream for tea at a wayside inn, and it had been in his company, after a thunderstorm, that Laura. for the only time in her life, had seen rose and mauve mountain-tints on the hills. Since then, as she afterwards learned, he had served four years with the fighting forces in France and had married and had children. But these experiences had had little effect upon his outward appearance. He had still the same sturdy figure, bright inquisitive eyes and head bent a little forward as though perpetually in search of news for his paper. He was scribbling in his notebook and did not look up as Laura passed by, her footsteps muffled by the road-dust.

Laura herself had not changed greatly in looks. A few grey hairs lurking among the brown, a neck less white and plump, and a new faint vertical line between the eyebrows, discernible by herself but as yet unnoticed by others, were nature's first gentle warning of approaching middle-age; but meanwhile she shared with other women of her age at that time the extension, if not of youth, of apparent youngishness, due to the recent revolution in fashions. The long heavy skirts, the elaborately coiled hair, the fussy trimmings and loaded hats of pre-war days had disappeared and a simpler style had emerged. In a neat, scantily cut costume with the skirt reaching but a little below the knee and a small, plain hat worn over bobbed hair, many a woman of forty looked younger than she had done at

---

[53] Almost certainly William Austen Sillick of the *Haslemere Herald*

[54] 12th May 1900: 'There is an element of mystery surrounding the death of a labourer named Albert Pannell, aged 35, whose body last week was found in Waggoners Wells'—*Haslemere Herald*

thirty. This style of dress had, as they said, 'caught on' and was popular with women of all ages; but the ease, comfort, and freedom of movement it gave could only be fully appreciated by those of an age to remember walking in the rain with a long skirt grabbed up in one hand lest the hem should get muddied and the other hand supporting an open umbrella to protect the built-up edifice of wired ribbon and artificial flowers then known as a hat.

Seeing a remembered name over a shop which also displayed a notice of 'Teas' to be had within, Laura entered. The woman who attended to her needs was one of the old Heatherley shopkeepers. She did not recognise Laura, which was not to be wondered at, as to her she must have been but one of many who had come there and gone without leaving behind any special cause for remembrance. When reminded by Laura that she had been a customer of hers of old, she said she had some faint recollection of sending her lunch to the post office. Did she not once complain of too much soda in some rock cakes? The former critic of rock cakes did her best to wipe out the memory of past indiscretion by praising the cake she was then eating and, finding Mrs Apsley willing to let bygones be bygones, enquired about a few of the people she had known in the village. Some were married, some dead, others had gone away to live in other places. Alma had married about the same time as Laura and was living away from Heatherley.[55] Except for Mrs Parkhurst, whom she had already seen, no one seemed to be left there in whom she had felt any particular interest.

"And of course," said Mrs Apsley, "you heard of that awful affair at the post office?" Laura had heard, or rather had read in the newspaper, that a few months after she left Heatherley[56] Mr Hertford had made a maniacal attack upon and killed his wife one morning as she was stooping over the bath in which was her newest baby. "Murder, committed under an uncontrollable impulse" had been the verdict of a humane jury, and the sentence had been detention during His Majesty's pleasure. Laura had pictured the village as it must have been that morning. The screaming and rushing to and fro; the village constable suddenly called upon to face what was almost certainly, to him, an unprecedented situation;

---

[55] Annie Symonds married Harold Chapman (Walter's nephew) on 12th January 1910, after which they ran the post office together in Beacon Hill, about a mile away

[56] The murder occurred on 29th July 1901

women running into their houses and locking their doors when they heard a madman was at large; other women forming a crowd outside the post office to watch the helpful few, called forth by any emergency, go in and out through the doorway; then the arrival of the closed carriage which was in use there, to take brides to their weddings and mourners to funerals, and the dazed culprit ushered into it, arm in arm with doctor and policeman, while all the time, but a few yards away, the sun shone on the heather, pine-tops swayed in the breeze, birds sang and bees gathered honey, as on any ordinary summer morning.

For some time Laura pictured that scene with horror during sleepless nights and days, haunted by misgivings as to whether there was anything she ought to have done, or anyone she should have told of the Hertfords' affairs, while she was living with them. Then, gradually, her horror and concern lessened, the sharpness and poignancy of the imagined scene softened and grew dim, and as the years flew by, bringing with them new responsibilities, new griefs and new experiences, the sorrow and tragedy of the Hertfords became to her but one of the sadder pages of memory.

By the time she revisited Heatherley "the awful affair at the post office" had, even to the inhabitants of the place, become an old story, and Mrs Apsley did not dwell upon it. The conversation turned to Heatherley's palmy days, when trade was good in the shops, boarding-houses were full, and famous men were to be seen walking its two streets. The celebrities who had lived there in Laura's time had died or gone away. Mrs Apsley said she thought two or three well-known people still lived on or near the hill, but you did not seem to hear as much about them as you would have done formerly; the war, she supposed, had altered ideas. Visitors still came to the hotels, though more of them to lunch or tea than for a longer stay, now that the motor-car had brought the place within easy reach of London. Since the war a new class of visitor had appeared, brought in crowds by the new motor-coaches for a day on the hill, and these, Mrs Apsley thought, had driven away what she called the better class of visitor. But she was quite tolerant of these new day visitors. When Laura said mildly that she supposed they enjoyed their outings, she said that she liked to see them enjoying themselves; they also brought a little money to the shops, and their money was as good as anybody else's; though she did wish they would not strew the place with orange-peel and paper bags. To show that she bore Laura no ill will for her long-ago criticism of her rock cakes, she not only brought a dish of water for her little dog, but also gave him a stale bun to eat, saying, "You must bring your mistress to see me again one of these days."

On her homeward way Laura came to the place on the heath where she had first seen heather in bloom. The hour was later than that in which she had first gazed on that scene and in place of rich golden sunshine a low, slanting light struck redly between the pine-trunks and cast long, searchlight rays on the heath; but, as then, the pale mauve of the heather misted hillock and dell and the bracken was turning from green to golden. The only apparent change was that a mountain ash which she had known as a slender sapling had grown stouter and taller and was hung with bright scarlet berries.

The little by-road appeared to be even less used than formerly. Before the day of the motorbus it had been a short cut to the main road and the town and railway station, but now, when everyone had that useful vehicle to command, pedestrians were seldom seen on any of the country roads and such by-roads as this were especially deserted. A notice affixed to the signpost at the turning declared it "Unsuitable for Motor Traffic", and it appeared to have been given over to rabbits and wagtails.

For a long time Laura stood in undisturbed contemplation. A grasshopper shrilled in a tuft at her feet and was answered by other shrillings among the gorse bushes; a solitary rook flapped heavily overhead, and a pair of goldfinches twittered among the thistledown; there was no other sound except the scarcely perceptible never-ceasing sighing of the wind in the pines and its rustling of acres of heath-bells.

When Laura had first looked upon that scene she had been young, with life, full of possibilities, stretching away before her; then, her heart had bounded and her nerves had thrilled with joy at the sight; she beheld it again as one whose youth had long ago fled and been followed by the better years of mature life, and the sight brought to her comfort and healing rather than joy. The intervening years had been crammed with the busy responsibilities, joys and anxieties, hopes and set-backs, inseparable from running a home and bringing up a family. Often, for months together, she had not been out of doors alone at a distance from home, as she was that evening. Now, standing apart, though but a short space apart in time or distance from her loved home ties, she was able, once again, to think of herself as an individual.

During the early years of her marriage, with her children small, her house to be kept as she liked it, and a very small income to be stretched to the utmost, she had had neither time nor inclination to think of herself apart; but of late, with her children growing up and less dependent upon her constant care, the old feeling had revived that in return for the precious opportunity known as life some further effort other than those involved in mere living was required of her. She had not entirely neglected to cultivate her one small gift of self-expression; short stories and articles of hers had been appearing occasionally for the past ten years in newspapers and women's weeklies. The remuneration for these had been a welcome addition to the family exchequer, but otherwise they amounted to little. It was not of writing small sugared love tales she had dreamed in her youth, and she had sometimes told herself with a somewhat wry smile, though not without enjoyment of the humour of the situation, that the pen she had taken for a sword had turned in her hands into a darning-needle.

She had heard or had read that every individual human life tends to move in cycles, that once and again we return to some previous starting point and are given a new opportunity. If that were so, she had that day completed one such cycle on the exact spot where her adult life had begun. What was to follow? A slackening and slowing down over the old course, or a new path, striking outward?

Notes on characters within Heatherley

Where we are certain of the names of people and places referred to by Flora Thompson in *Heatherley*, they are shown as footnotes in the body of the book. The following notes relate to:—

- people about whom we have not yet obtained conclusive proof, although we are reasonably confident of their identity, *or*
- circumstances or events which require more space to explain than would reasonably fit in a footnote.

Mr Charles Foreshaw

There are few positive clues as to who 'Mr Foreshaw' might have been. However, Flora does indicate that he was buried locally, and only one man in the surrounding parishes' burial records seems to come close to fitting his description. This is John Volckman, who died on 10th August 1900, aged 63, and was buried in the church-yard at All Saints, Headley. The note against his name in the register states: *'of 3 Chichester Street, St. George's Square, London SW—Stranger at Grayshott—friend is A.L. Pike.'*

An obituary in the *Surrey Advertiser* adds the information that the Rev J.M. Jeakes of Grayshott officiated and the chief mourners included Miss Volckman (sister), Mr Arthur L Pike (nephew), and Mr H.A. Swepstone (solicitor to the deceased).

Bob and Jeanette Pikesley

Who 'Bob Pikesley' and his sister 'Jeanette' really were, we may never know—indeed they could well be composite characters built from a number of people whom Flora had met at different times in her life. But she does give us a clue. When living in Liphook, she says she was told that 'Jeanette' had nursed her old mother through her last illness and looked after the house and dairy, then both she and 'Bob' had died "in that influenza epidemic, as they called it, just after the war. Both down with it at the same time and nobody to look after them."

Local burial records show only one pair of people dying of the post-war 'flu within days of each other, this being Albert Alderton and his wife Emily, who both died of 'flue & pneumonia' in February 1919 according to the Headley register. He was 51 and she 47 years old, and they lived in Whitmore Vale, a narrow, tree-lined valley which fits almost exactly Flora's description of where the 'Pikesley' farm was. To add to this evidence, the Rector's notes also state that Emily had been looking after her mother during a long illness just before she died.

If the Aldertons really were Flora's 'Bob and Jeanette,' then they were not brother and sister as she described, but husband and wife.

Children of Walter and Emily Chapman

When Flora first knew the 'Hertfords' they had, as she says, a boy and a girl. The boy Walter George, to whom Flora refers as 'Cecil,' was aged 3½ and the girl, Florence Louise (known in the family as 'Lulu'), was nearly 2 years old. Another boy and girl were born while she was there (although Flora herself mentions only the girl)—these were Thomas Gillman born on 1st March 1899, and Ethel on 6th June 1900. And finally, Ernest James was born on 16th June 1901, after Flora had left the village.

Richard and Mavis Brownlow

It is likely that the real 'Richard Brownlow,' was William Burton Elwes. He had joined *Cable & Wireless* in 1894, and served them in Singapore, Madras and Hong Kong before returning to a home posting in 1922. He retired as Staff Controller on 30th March 1937 at the age of fifty-nine, and both his photograph at that time and the description of him moving to 'a Georgian cottage overlooking a lovely valley' in Pett, East Sussex fit Flora's description of 'Richard.'

Furthermore, the grandniece of William Elwes is struck by Flora's description of 'Richard' first entering her post office—particularly the clear eyes, fair skin, and cheeks whipped into rosiness; also his love of countryside and an interest in knowing the right names for everything, and his concern about social injustice, but no plans for doing anything about it. "That's Uncle Bill!" she said.

But there were other parts of the story which did not fit. For one thing, their father had not died suddenly—he had in fact been an Archdeacon in Madras, and died in 1924 at the age of 80. Also, William Elwes' sister Lilian was tall and elegant with blue eyes, not as Flora described 'Mavis.' She had never suffered from tuberculosis, and would not have considered doing anything so menial as working for a living. The family at that time, on the admission of today's generation, were 'a bit snobbish.'

'Uncle Bill' had been known as a 'bit of a flirt,' his grandniece tells us, and was in demand with the ladies—but apparently always had to get the approval of his sister before starting anything serious! And this might be the key to our conundrum. Flora, it seems, is unlikely to have been regarded as sufficiently 'top drawer' for the Elwes family at the time, and if Bill's flirting with her began to look as if it was getting beyond a casual affair, Lilian may well have decided to put a stop to it. If so, then the excuse of 'Mavis' having an illness as the reason for 'Richard' pulling out could have been fabricated, either by Flora or by 'Richard,' to save face.

William Austen Sillick

The reporter was almost certainly William Austen Sillick, who at the age of twenty-one was the sole local representative for the *Haslemere Herald* during the time that Flora was in Grayshott.

He was also an enthusiastic compiler of notes on the eminent people of the area. In Haslemere Museum, there is a lovingly gathered collection of newspaper cuttings and jottings of his, and a notebook in which he recorded information specifically about the personalities who lived in and around Grayshott.

How ironic, then, that it includes no mention of the young girl he had walked with on the heaths, and sat with for hours by Waggoners Wells. But how could he have known then that, one day, she also would be worthy of a place in his collection?

For further reading …

On the Trail of Flora Thompson by John Owen Smith.
ISBN 1-873855-24-9

This is a delightful book that goes behind the scenes, as it were, of the author of *Lark Rise to Candleford*. It is aptly sub-titled *Beyond Candleford Green.* —Graham Collyer, Editor *Surrey Advertiser*

John Owen Smith, publisher as well as author, has done a marvellous research job in unveiling her life during these years; what makes his story all the more interesting is that he takes his readers with him through his exhaustive enquiries and interviews, so that at times it has the suspense of a who-dunnit.

In addition, it is beautifully illustrated with old photographs and even suggested walks in Flora's footsteps. A lovely book.
—Colin Dunne, Editor *Downs Country*

Books of local interest by the same publisher

One Monday in November—the story of the Selborne and
Headley Workhouse Riots of 1830
During the 'Swing' riots of 1830, according to the famed historians
J.L. and Barbara Hammond, "the most interesting event in the
Hampshire rising was the destruction of the workhouses at Selborne
and Headley." If these riots had succeeded, "the day when the
Headley workhouse was thrown down would be remembered ... as
the day of the taking of the Bastille." Here a local historian traces
the dramatic events of two days of rioting and its aftermath in the
villages and beyond.

From the Preface to **One Monday in November**:
John Owen Smith's book is a real contribution to our history. It
tells the story of a few tragic days in East Hampshire in 1830,
when hungry men, bewildered by falling wages and rising prices,
blundered into mob action ....

I am particularly happy to have the chance to introduce the book
to the public. A few years ago I researched and wrote a brief
account of the riots, so I am probably one of the few people who
can appreciate fully how hard Mr Smith must have worked, how
thorough and widespread his investigations have been, unearthing
ten times more information than I found. He gives us the economic
and social background and then recounts the facts, with clarity,
humour and impartiality. His sympathies are clear, but he has not
made all his rich men villains or all his poor men saints; he has
told it "as it happened". Selborne, Headley and Liphook are much
in his debt.

L.C.Giles
Vice-Chairman, Bramshott and Liphook Preservation Society

ISBN 1-873855-09-5 May 1993 Paperback, A4 landscape,
40pp, illustrations plus maps.

RIOT! or This Bloody Crew—an historical drama
The stage script of the Workhouse Riots story, performed as a
community play in October 1993. Includes historical notes.
ISBN 1-873855-01-X November 1993 Paperback, A4 landscape,
36pp, illustrations plus maps.
   (Also available on audio cassette as adapted for radio)

Books of local interest by the same publisher (contd)

*A Balance of Trust—The foundation of The National Trust
and 50 years of history in & around Haslemere, 1855-1905*
Haslemere was, quite literally, on the road to nowhere until the
railway arrived in 1859 and opened up the area as a commuter belt.
Ready access to and from London then put pressure on the
surrounding common land, giving in-comers incentives to buy and
to build. In short, the area was earmarked for invasion.

One such commuter was Sir Robert Hunter, legal adviser to the
Post Office, whose vision of the need to secure and protect land of
natural beauty for the nation created The National Trust.

From his base in Haslemere we are introduced to events and
characters of national significance. Famed for its healthy air, the
area soon became the haunt of writers, artists, politicians and
scientists of repute. People such as Alfred Lord Tennyson, Helen
Allingham and Sir Arthur Conan Doyle were all active in the
neighbourhood, and we follow their contribution to the debates of
the time. Flora Thompson was there too.

Illustrated throughout with many photographs of the period, it
will appeal to those interested in the National Trust, the postal
service, great literary characters, 'Green' issues, and the fate of
threatened open spaces such as Hindhead Common today.
*ISBN 1-873855-12-5 Sep 1995 Paperback, A4 landscape,
60pp, period illustrations plus maps.*

Some Ancient Churches in North East Hampshire
—an illustrated collection of notes
Twelve fascinating churches in the north east corner of Hampshire
are described. A map on the back cover guides you through the
picturesque lanes of the area, and 33 photographs give both exterior
and interior views of each church. Villages include Bentley ("The
Village" of TV & Radio), Selborne of Gilbert White fame, East
Worldham with the body of Chaucer's wife, Binsted where
Montgomery of Alamein lies, and Bramshott, the final resting place
for so many Canadian servicemen of the First World War. A short
glossary is included for those unfamiliar with some of the architec-
tural terms used. Suitable size for the pocket.
*ISBN 1-873855-11-7 April 1995 Paperback, A5 portrait,
28pp, illustrations plus map.*

Books of local interest by the same publisher (contd)

All Tanked Up—*the Canadians in Headley during World War II*
A story of the benign 'invasion' of a Hampshire village by Canadian tank regiments over a period of four years, told from the point of view of both Villagers and Canadians. Includes technical details of tanks, and full Order of Battle for Canadian Regiments in 1945, as well as many personal reminiscences.
ISBN 1-873855-00-1 May 1994 Paperback, A4 landscape, 48pp, illustrations plus maps.

Flora Thompson on Stage

The publisher of this book has written stage plays covering the two periods of Flora Thompson's life in East Hampshire.

In *Flora's Heatherley* we see her arrive as a young, gauche country girl and pass, as she says, "from foolish youth to wicked adolescence" in Grayshott. This play examines the conventions of the period, particularly with respect to courtship and marriage, and Flora's difficulty in conforming to them.
First performed in September 1998.

In *Flora's Peverel* we see her fifteen years later, as a married lady with a husband and children of her own. This play brings to life the period in Liphook when, against the odds, she "won the fight to write" as a contemporary of hers put it.
First performed in May 1997.

For details and performance rights of both these plays, contact the publisher at the address shown in this book.

John Owen Smith, *publisher*:—
Tel/Fax: (01428) 712892
E-mail: wordsmith@headley1.demon.co.uk
Web Site: www.headley1.demon.co.uk/

Index